LITURGY
OF THE WORD FOR
CHILDREN

Alison Travers

Foreword by Bishop David Konstant

McCRIMMONS
Great Wakering   Essex

First published in Great Britain in 1986 by
McCrimmon Publishing Co Ltd
Great Wakering Essex England

© 1986 Sr Alison Travers

ISBN 0 85597 387 0

Typeset and printed in Hong Kong by
Permanent Typesetting & Printing Co Ltd

To the children and catechists of St Augustine's Parish, Milton Keynes.

Acknowledgements

I wish to express my thanks to Fr Geoffrey Burke, of Forest Row, for giving us the idea of a Children's Liturgy of the Word; Fr Michael Turner and Fr James Cassidy, who encouraged me to get started; Fr Paul Hardy, Miss Maire Crowson and the many parent-catechists who have given me valuable ideas while providing a sounding board for my own; and the parishioners who helped me with the typing and retyping as the scheme developed.

Extracts from the *Jerusalem Bible*, published and copyright 1966, 1967 and 1968 by Darton, Longman and Todd and Doubleday & Co Inc, are used by permission of the publishers. Extracts from the *Good News Bible*, © American Bible Society 1976, published by The Bible Societies and Collins, are used by permission. Extracts from *New World* © Oxford University Press, 1967. Reprinted for *New World* by Alan T Dale (1967) by permission of Oxford University Press. Extracts from *Listen! Themes from the Bible*, by AJ McCallen, © Collins Publishers, 8 Grafton Street, London W1X 3LA, are used by permission. Christmas Time is Coming, Advent Song and Question and Answer Carol from *Let God's Children Sing* by Sister Mary Oswin, published by Geoffrey Chapman. Used by permission.

Contents

Foreword 5
Introduction 7
Notes for Sundays up to Christ the King 9
Autumn term: Sundays up to Christ the King 9
Jesus calls us to be his followers 10
We follow Jesus: What kind of a person is he? 11
Jesus loves children and likes to be with them 12
Jesus calls us to grow in love 13
Jesus asks his followers to trust him 14
Jesus wants his followers to be generous 15
Jesus wants his followers to help each other 16
Jesus accepts us—whoever we are 17
The saints are people who grow like Jesus 18
Jesus wants his followers to forgive 19
Sunday before the Feast of Christ the King 21
Celebration for Christ the King 22
Notes for Advent 23
Advent 1: Light 24
Advent 2: Preparation 25
Advent 3: The message 26
Advent 4: Presents 27
Notes for Sundays after Christmas 29
The Wise Men come to Jesus 29
The Baptism of Jesus: A celebration 31
We live our Baptism by trying to live like Jesus 32
Jesus teaches his followers to pray 34
Our Father: Session One 34
Our Father: Session Two 35
Our Father: Session Three 36
Notes for Lent 37
Sunday before Lent 39
First Sunday in Lent 41
Second Sunday in Lent 43
Third Sunday in Lent 45
Fourth Sunday in Lent 47
Fifth Sunday in Lent 48
Notes for Eastertide 49
Easter celebration 51
Easter 3: Jesus comes to his friends 52
Easter 4: Jesus and Thomas 53
Easter 5: The Good Shepherd 54
Easter 6: The lakeside meal 55
Easter 7: The secret of happiness 56
Life and growth 58
Celebration of life and growth 59
Notes for Whitsuntide 60
Pentecost 61
Pentecost 2 62

Contents (continued)

Pentecost 3 63
Pentecost 4 64
Pentecost 5 66
Pentecost 6 67
Pentecost 7 69
Pentecost 8 70
Music 72

Preface

Required for the scheme:

Good News Version, New Testament;

New World, Alan Dale, OUP;

Listen! Themes From the Bible, A J McCallen, Collins;

Stations of the Cross pictures, Vita et Pax, 1979, available from McCrimmon Publishing Co Ltd.

Suggested:

Praise!, A J McCallen, Collins;

Complete Celebration Hymnal (CCH), Mayhew McCrimmon Ltd;

Songs of the Spirit (SOS), Kevin Mayhew Ltd;

William Barclay's commentaries on Mark, Luke, Matthew (vol 2), John (vol 2), Acts, in the *Daily Study Bible* series, St Andrew Press;

Stations of the Cross, Peter Cullen, Mayhew-McCrimmon Ltd;

Getting to Know About series, Denholm House Press: *Farming and Fishing; Festivals;*

New Testament Catechetical Posters, LDC, Italy, obtainable from St Paul's Book Centre;

Acclaim the King (AK), McCrimmon Publishing Co Ltd.

Foreword

In leading children to worship we need to find the right balance between treating them as a special group and accepting them as members of the whole community. They are both of course: they are a special group of people with their own needs, and at the same time they should belong as fully as possible to the whole family of believers which is the parish.

When it comes to the celebration of Sunday Mass the balance is not always easy to find. The Liturgy of the Eucharist speaks particularly by signs, and in any case is part of family worship in which young and old take part together. The young child's needs in this area are related to a sense of belonging and of wonder rather than to understanding. But the Liturgy of the Word is different. Here is an activity which is both worship and catechesis. This means that we should make real efforts to help them understand what is happening and being said as a means to their growing in faith.

For those still too young to appreciate the meaning and richness of the readings and homily at the Sunday Mass, a Liturgy of the Word and a catechesis appropriate to their needs and abilities is ideal. This book offers just the sort of guidance the catechist of young children may want. The careful selection of readings, the explanations for the catechist, the suggestions for bidding prayers and celebrations will, I believe, prove immediately helpful. I am delighted that Sister Alison has, after many years' experience of this work with children, put pen to paper for the benefit of us all.

+ David Konstant
Bishop of Leeds

Introduction

Why have a Liturgy of the Word for Children?

I still get asked this question. The answer lies in Vatican II's Document on the Liturgy which states:

1. 'Mother church earnestly desires that *all* the faithful be led to that full, conscious and active participation in liturgical celebrations which is demanded by the very nature of liturgy.'
2. 'This full and active participation by all the people is the aim to be considered *before all else*; for it (the sacred liturgy) is the primary and indispensable source from which the faithful are to derive the true christian spirit.' (14) (The italics are mine)

Have we, in this country, taken these words of the Council seriously? If we wish children to worship with their parents on a Sunday, are children's Masses the answer? How far can primary school children participate fully and consciously in the adult Liturgy of the Word? How far can the Sunday readings and homily be the source of the christian spirit for them? As our parish priest succinctly remarked: 'By keeping children in church during the adult Liturgy of the Word, we are effectively teaching them to switch off.'

It was with thoughts such as these in mind that we decided six years ago to start a Liturgy of the Word for children at our main Sunday Mass.

The advantages of a Liturgy of the Word for Children

Children are able to participate in the same Mass as their parents while receiving the Word of God at their own level. They can be led to full, conscious and active participation because God's Word is chosen with their needs in view; it is related to their experience, and they are encouraged to share their ideas in discussion. They can make up their own Bidding Prayers, and the Act of Faith, flowing from their discussion, can have real meaning for them. The liturgy can become the source of the true christian spirit if children feel they have their part to play, understand what they are doing and enjoy the celebration. Parents remark that children no longer groan at the idea of going to Mass because they experience the Eucharist as a joyful event.

Material

At the beginning we followed the Sunday Gospels, using a simplified version. We found, however, that many of the Gospels were unsuitable for young children and the Lectionary did not provide us with the sequence we were looking for. After searching unsuccessfully for published material, I decided to write my own scheme for the seven to ten-year-olds. This book is Year One of a two-year scheme. It follows the liturgical cycle and was written very specifically with our own situation in mind. I offered it for publication because so many people have approached me asking for help and saying they would start a Liturgy of the Word for Children if they could find a suitable scheme.

Use of the scheme

Every parish situation is different and I offer this scheme as a *guideline* enabling catechists to branch out on their own. The notes for each session are very full but I was asked not to shorten them. Catechists who feel unsure at the beginning find full notes give them confidence; catechists who have found their feet appreciate the breadth of choice offered.

The format for each Sunday is the same:

Points for the catechist
Reading
Presentation
Act of Faith
Bidding Prayers

Within this framework, while adhering to the Reading, catechists should feel free to use their own ideas. A scheme has to be general whereas the catechist can use topical incidents from family life, from local events or from international news. Hymns can be chosen by the children and Bidding Prayers will often arise naturally from the session.

Points for the catechist

These have been written to provide background material at adult level. They have been kept short because we use William Barclay's Commentaries on the Gospels which we find invaluable. Although written by a scripture scholar, they are easy to read; they have a devotional aspect, and provide excellent background material on such things as Palestinian shepherds, storms on the Sea of Galilee, tax collecting, etc. Most of our catechists have brought their own copies of Mark and Luke, and the parish lends out the other commentaries.

Reading and response

The Reading has been typed in for each session; but for greater solemnity the catechist should read the Gospel direct from *New World*, *Listen* or the *Good News* New Testament. It is often helpful to intersperse the reading with comments, or to have a short introduction. Sometimes I ask the children to listen carefully so that they can share with the group what they like best in the Gospel, or what they consider to be the Good News. There are no right or wrong answers in this approach, which is encouraging!

The Response to the Good News is meant to be joyful. Children are not the only ones who need reminding of this!

Dramatisation and mime

I am a great believer in drama and mime, and many of the stories in the scheme lend themselves to this. Children are able to get under the skin of the characters they act, and in this way they can identify with the feelings of Jesus, the apostles, the people in the story. On the whole the scheme is cerebral and dramatisation provides a balance. We may appear to cover less ground but almost certainly the children will receive more from the session. It is not necessary to be a good actor or producer. What is needed is for the catechist to feel at ease with the group so that discipline doesn't break down!

Celebrations

These are important because they speak to the heart rather than to the head. I usually lead our celebrations because the groups join together and we may have as many as fifty children; but other catechists are encouraged to join in, and they are very joyful events.

Who can be a catechist?

The answer to this is anyone who has a love and understanding of children, a love of their own Faith, and the desire to pass it on. We have twenty-six catechists, the majority of whom are parents with no teaching experience. The number is large because we have two Mass centres and four catechists to each group of children.

I appreciate that one catechist to a group has certain advantages. However, we find that with four to a group no parent misses the adult readings and homily more than once a month, the groups are never without a catechist, and each adult has his or her own special gifts and insights to offer.

For continuity of approach it is important to have regular meetings. Meetings also enable catechists to see the scheme as a whole. They provide an opportunity for sharing insights, and give new catechists valuable support.

From time to time problems of discipline may arise and can be sorted out! Because our numbers are large I act as co-ordinator; but this could be someone from within each group.

One practical point: it is helpful if each catechist has a date list and the telephone numbers of the others in the group.

Where do these liturgies take place?

In the church we use the sacristy (with children sitting on a carpet), the weekday chapel, a priest's office with little ones bulging into the passage, and another small room. A small altar, ie a table with a white cloth, crucifix and candle, is a remainder to the children that they are still at Mass doing at their level what their parents are doing in church.

The time element

Where possible much is gained by the children leaving the church at the beginning of Mass. If, as in our situation, the church gets congested, they may have to remain with their parents until after the opening prayer, to ensure having a seat. Before the readings start, the priest gives the 'Book' to one child and the others in the group process out behind it. At the Creed an altar boy lets the catechists know, and they draw the session to a close. The children return to their places with the Procession of the Gifts.

Follow-up

During Lent and Advent, and on some other occasions, we give the children something definite to do at home.

If a summary of the material covered in the session is printed in the weekly newsletter, parents can follow up the work done in the group.

Occasional meetings for parents who have children attending these Liturgies of the Word are also useful.

A final point

I am aware that this scheme leaves much to be desired. It will have achieved its aim if it proves a starting point for those who wish to have a Liturgy of the Word for Children and have felt unable to begin for lack of material.

Notes for Sundays up to Christ the King

1. It is important to read the scheme through so that it is seen as a whole rather than as a series of isolated incidents. The theme— Jesus calls us to follow Him—aims at helping children to understand the kind of person Jesus is and the kind of people he wants us to be. It is important therefore to relate the readings to the children's experience.

2. Because these stories are so familiar, try to read them afresh, pondering their meaning in your own life, before reading the notes or Barclay's commentary. With the children try to draw out their understanding before imposing your own. They will often shed new and unexpected light on the readings.

3. Asking questions and dealing with answers is an art which develops as we become familiar with a group of children. It is important to accept their answers, however strange they may be. Responses such as: 'That's interesting.' 'I hadn't thought of that.' 'Has any one any other ideas?' will encourage children who lack confidence. Never make a child appear foolish.

4. In miracle stories stress the healing rather than the miraculous aspect. Jesus is not a magician or superman. His miracles never stop at the purely physical level. The word used for miracle by St John is SIGN and Jesus' miracles are signs of God's love and power at work in the world; signs of the coming of God's Kingdom.

5. Parables were a favourite form of teaching. The picture story is easily remembered, but the listener has to think out the meaning. There is usually one point to a parable, and we have often missed the essential meaning by reading too much into them. They can be deceptively simple. Children are more likely to understand them through drama than from much explanation.

6. *Praise!* and *Listen!* both have useful alternative material for the Act of Faith.

Autumn term
Sundays up to Christ the King

Jesus calls us to follow Him

Sunday One: Jesus calls us to follow him. Call of Matthew.

Sunday Two: We follow Jesus. What kind of a person is he? A Day in the life of Jesus.

Sunday Three: Jesus loves children and likes to be with them. Jesus makes the children welcome.

Sunday Four: Jesus calls us to grow in love. God makes everything grow.

Sunday Five: Jesus asks his followers to trust him. Jesus looks after a little girl.

Sunday Six: Jesus wants his followers to be generous. The poor old woman.

Sunday Seven: Jesus wants his followers to help each other. The man who came through the roof.

Sunday Eight: Jesus accepts us whoever we are. Jesus heals the leper.

Sunday Nine: The Saints are people who grow like Jesus. What Love really means.

Sunday Ten: Jesus wants his followers to forgive. Parable of the unforgiving servant.

Sunday Eleven: Preparation for the Feast of Christ the King.

Sunday Twelve: Celebration for the Feast of Christ the King.

Jesus calls us to be his followers

READING: Call of Matthew, *Listen* (p146), No 73, Mark 2: 13–17.

One day Jesus met a man called Matthew, who was a tax collector. He was sitting in his house working when Jesus came, but Jesus said: 'Follow me!' and Matthew got up at once and followed him.

Then he took Jesus for a meal and he invited a lot of his friends as well. Some of the teachers saw this and they said: 'Matthew's old friends are bad people. Why does Jesus go and eat with them?'. But Jesus heard them saying this and said: 'I have come to *help* bad people, that's why. I can't help the people who think they're all right.'

POINTS FOR CATECHIST

Barclay on Mark 2: 13–17.

The emphasis is on Jesus' call and Matthew's response. Jesus called his apostles not just for their own benefit, but *to share in his work*. He calls us at our baptism in the same way. He came to save *all* men, and like speaks to like; so he chose his apostles from different walks of life, men of very different temperaments. Jesus looks to the heart and does not choose as we would choose.

PRESENTATION

1. Reading.

2. Who was Matthew? Describe shortly the work of a tax collector in those days.

   What kind of a person was Matthew? Discuss. Greedy—thinking of his own gain? Thoughtless—simply following his father's trade? Unable to get any other job?

   How did Matthew respond to Jesus' call? Left everything immediately, joyfully; shared his joy with his friends. (Party.) Why did Jesus call Matthew? (Be his friend, work for him.) Why did he *choose* Matthew? What did he see in him? Would you have chosen him?

Did Matthew always manage to follow Jesus perfectly? (Wasn't with him at the crucifixion.) Jesus simply asks his friends to do their best.

3. Jesus called each one of us to follow him? When? (Baptism.) Why did he call us? Did he call us because we were clever, nice, good.....? Discuss.

   How does he call us each day—in what ways? How do we respond? Slowly—eagerly—joyfully—miserably, etc.

   Some people were angry at Jesus' choice of Matthew, and said nasty things. Are we ever upset when someone else is chosen to do something?

4. What did Jesus mean: 'I have come to help bad people, I can't help the people who think they're all right'?

ACT OF FAITH:

Lord Jesus, may we come to know you more clearly,
   To love you more dearly,
   and to follow you more nearly,
   day by day.

or Hymn, *CCH* 76, 'Follow Christ and love the world'.

BIDDING PRAYERS (Response: Lord Jesus, please bless them)

We pray for those who are learning to be priests and nuns.

We pray for people who are learning to become Christians.

We pray for those who go to foreign countries to teach people about Jesus.

We follow Jesus: What kind of a person is he?

READING: A day in the life of Jesus, *New World*, pages 6 & 8 (adapted). Mark 1: 21, 22, 29–39.

Jesus and his friends were in Capernaum, a fishing town on the shores of Galilee Lake. It was Saturday, the Holy Day of the Jews, and Jesus and his friends went along to the Meeting House and took part in the service of worship. Jesus began to teach and the people who heard him were amazed at the way he taught.

Jesus and his friends left the building and went along with James and John to the home of Peter and Andrew. Peter's mother-in-law was in bed with fever. They told Jesus about her, and he went to her and took hold of her hand and lifted her up. The fever left her and she looked after the visitors.

At sunset, when the Holy Day was over, people brought all who were ill in body or mind to Jesus. The whole town crowded round the door of the house. Jesus made them all better, whatever their illness was.

Early next morning, while it was still dark, Jesus got up and went out of the house to a lonely place. Peter and his friends hunted him out and found him—praying.

'Everybody's looking for you,' they told him. But Jesus said: 'We must go on to the other villages round here. I have to preach in them also.'

POINTS FOR CATECHIST

Read Barclay on Mark 1: 21, 22; 29–39.

It would be wise at this age level to leave out passages on devil possession. The emphasis is on the person of Jesus. This passage, often called 'A day in the life of Jesus', shows us how he spends his time. As adults we need to stop and think, Who is Jesus for me?

PRESENTATION

1. Reading.

2. What is Jesus doing at the beginning and at the end of the passage? Sharing in the religious practices of his people and teaching (preaching the homily). You could explain briefly how our Liturgy of the Word is patterned on the Synagogue service—hymn (psalms), reading, homily, prayers.

Jesus always found time to pray, even at the end of a busy day. Do we?

3. Discuss how he spent his day with his friends in an ordinary family. (Remember any other family like this?—Martha and Mary.) His influence on others—when he healed Granny, she got up and looked after the family and visitors. In Holy Communion Jesus comes to us to help us to grow like him—thinking of others. How did Jesus feel at the *end* of the day when the crowds brought the sick to him? He could have slipped away saying 'I'm tired... I'm busy....' How do we feel when we come home from school and are asked to help? People brought their troubles to Jesus because they trusted him and he showed that he cared. Can we share our troubles with Jesus? Do we?

PRESENTATION, 7–8 YEARS

Either adapt the above or tell the story of Jesus healing Peter's mother-in-law (granny) in your own words. Granny gets ill—the worry—running to Jesus for help, knowing he'd be at worship on the Sabbath, bringing him home—the bustle and sorrow—Jesus' quiet, gentle sureness, granny sitting up, 'What's all the fuss?', fussing around the pots and pans, joyful meal.

ACT OF FAITH (Response: We believe.)

We believe God is our loving Father
We believe he sent Jesus to show us how to live
We believe in the Holy Spirit who lives in us and helps us.

or Hymn, *CCH* 99 'God's Spirit is in my heart', verse 1 and chorus.

BIDDING PRAYERS (Lord Jesus, please bless them)

We pray for people who cannot get to Mass on Sundays because they are sick.

We pray for all grannies and grandpas.

We pray for anyone we know in hospital.

Jesus loves children and likes to be with them

READING: *Listen* (Page 64) No 30, Jesus makes the children welcome. Mark 10: 13–16.

People often used to bring children to Jesus. When they did, Jesus always gave them his blessing. One day, however, some of the friends of Jesus told the children to go away. Jesus was angry when he saw this happening and he said:
'Don't stop the children from coming to me. Don't send them away like that! Bring them back.'
Then he put his arms round the children and he blessed them.

POINTS FOR THE CATECHIST

Read Barclay's Commentary on Mark 10: 10–16.
The message is that Jesus loves children and accepts them as they are. Has he a message here for us adults? He is not extolling childishness but the childlike qualities of trust, love and simplicity seen in very young children. He always had *time* for children.

PRESENTATION

1. Read the passage.

2. How do the children feel when adults have no time for them; don't listen properly, don't understand their feelings? Do they ever feel excluded by grown ups—ever feel in the way? Do they ever exclude others?—the slow, handicapped, unpopular, newcomers?

3. Help them reflect on their experience of an adult who always has time, listens to them, makes them feel wanted. Are they nicer to each other when with this person? Jesus was like this. He loved children, listened, made them feel wanted... How did children feel with him? (safe, happy—shared secrets with him, trusted him...).

Jesus wants *us* to share our joys, upsets, etc, with him. Discuss what we can share with him—how the day has gone—difficulty with our work—unfairly treated etc.

When can we share with Jesus?—in bed—after Holy Communion are special times; but we can talk to him at any time—ask for his help.

4. What were the children like whom Jesus welcomed? Well behaved—clean—tidy—'good'—rowdy, boisterous, awkward, slow, shy, clever, stupid—he welcomed all.

Could have been beggar children, a spastic, or blind child, a foreigner in the group.

Would he allow any to be left out?

How did the children behave with Jesus? —On best behaviour—or just themselves?

'Jesus blessed them'—What do you think this means?

ACT OF FAITH (Response: We love you and we trust you.)

Jesus, You always have time for us.
Jesus, you are always ready to forgive us.
Jesus, you want us to be kind to each other.
Jesus, you want to come to us in Holy Communion.
Or Hymn, *CCH* 84 'Give me joy'; *CCH* 292, 'Suffer little children'.

BIDDING PRAYERS (Dear Jesus, please bless them)

1. We pray for children who have physical handicaps.

2. We pray for children who find school work difficult.

3. We pray for children who have lost a mother or a father.

4. We pray for children who are unpopular.

Jesus calls us to grow in love

READING: *Listen* (Page 19), No 5B, God makes every thing grow. Mark 4: 26–29.

One day Jesus said:

The farmer goes out
and plants the seeds in his field.
But then he leaves them there
to grow all by themselves.

He doesn't understand HOW they grow
—he only knows they do—
even while he is asleep at night.

All of a sudden a little shoot appears
then it grows larger
and then the corn is there
all fully grown.

Then Jesus said: That is the way God works.

POINTS FOR CATECHIST

Read Barclay's Commentary on Mark 4: 26–9.

At baptism God plants the seed of his life and love in our hearts. He offers us all that we need for this seed to grow but we have to work with him. Growth of any kind is hard work. We speak of 'growing pains'.

PRESENTATION

1. Read the passage. Explain that it is a parable.

2. Jesus is talking about growth. Plants and animals grow and so do we.
   Are you different now from when you started school? How?—size—physical growth—things you can do—mental growth—way you treat people—growth in love.
   Can you *see* growth taking place—in nature, in yourself, your hair, nails, etc?

3. What do we need for growth?
   (1) Physical—food, drink, exercise, rest, play, LOVE....
   (2) Mental—imitation, hard work, listening, practice—in reading, writing, maths, sewing, etc. We have to *exercise* our minds and *use* our five senses.
   (3) Growth in love—we have first to ex-

perience being loved. Babies have to be nursed, cuddled, kissed, played with. Children have to be corrected, praised, shown love, forgiven.

We learn to use our ears and eyes to notice people's needs, and our voices to speak kindly, our minds to think HOW we can help and our hands to do things for others.

4. Some people have bodies that don't grow but their minds grow and their love grows.
   Others have minds that don't grow but their bodies grow and their love grows.
   Others have bodies and minds that grow but their love does not grow.
   What kind of growth is the most important?

5. How do we feed the seed of God's love within us? *By trying to grow like Jesus*

   By prayer—listening to Jesus, talking to him, asking his help.

   By listening—when we are taught about Jesus.

   By worshipping with God's family.

   By receiving Jesus in Holy Communion.

   By receiving forgiveness and help in the Sacrament of Reconciliation.

   By trying to imitate Jesus in his unselfishness, generosity, kindness, forgiveness.

   Growing like Jesus is hard work—but God is helping us all the time.

ACT OF FAITH

CCH 11 'All that I am...'; *CCH* 51 'Come, Lord Jesus, come'.

PRAYER

Dear Jesus,
may we come to know you more clearly
love you more dearly
and follow you more nearly
day by day.

Jesus asks his followers to trust him

READING: Jesus looks after a little girl, *Listen* (Page 66), No 31A. Mark 5: 21–24; 35–42.

One day a man called Jairus came to Jesus and threw himself down in front of him. 'My little girl is dying,' he said. 'Come and hold her in your arms and she will get better again.' So Jesus went along with him.

Then someone came and said: 'It's no use bothering Jesus any more. Your little girl has died.' But Jesus took no notice, and said to Jairus: 'Don't worry. All you have to do is to trust me.'

When they got to Jairus' house, there were lots of people there, and they were all crying. So Jesus said: 'What's all this for? the little girl isn't dead, she's only asleep.' But no one believed him. In fact, they even laughed at him.

So Jesus sent everyone out of the house. Then he went into the room where the little girl was lying, and he took with him only her mother and father, and Peter, James and John.

Then he held the girl's hand, and said: 'Get up, little girl.' And she did, and walked round the room. Her father and mother were so surprised, they just didn't know what to do, so Jesus told them to give the girl something to eat.

POINTS FOR CATECHIST

Barclay's Commentary on Mark 5: 21–4, 35–42.

Jesus wants us to trust him. The emphasis is on Jairus' trust in Jesus. Jesus says: 'I'm here. Everything will be all right.'

In Jewish custom, Jairus was an important official far superior to Jesus. For him to approach Jesus for help, therefore, showed great courage, humility and faith. Was it Jesus' own confidence in his Father which enabled people like Jairus to trust in him?

Jewish mourning customs are described well by Barclay. Often today we prevent people from mourning and expect them to hide their feelings. Yet to express our feelings and talk about someone who has died is a healing process.

PRESENTATION

1. Reading.
2. There is great scope for dramatising this story. It would help children enter into the feelings of the different people involved. If it is not acted, let the children discuss how the different people must have felt.

   Jairus—His love for his daughter—great distress—trust in Jesus.

   His friends—perhaps scoffing at him for asking Jesus for help.

   The sadness of the servants and crowd.

   Jesus' quiet serenity and authority. How did he feel?

   The great feeling of happiness at the end.

3. Discuss Jewish mourning customs. Many Eastern countries still keep similar customs. People in our country wear black. But the church sometimes uses white vestments for a requiem Mass as a sign of our hope in the resurrection of the dead.

4. At the end of the story, what tells us that Jesus understood the needs of children? (Give her something to eat). How did her parents feel? How do you think the little girl felt? How do you feel when you are ill, and someone helps you to get better? When you feel miserable, and that nobody loves you, do you ever turn to Jesus?

PRESENTATION, 7–8 YEARS.

Children will learn the meaning of this incident best by acting it. Do not go into the mourning customs unless a child asks about them. Otherwise adapt the above.

ACT OF FAITH

Jesus, we believe you are always ready to help us when we turn to you. We thank you for your help.

or Hymn, *CCH* 259 v3, 'Trust Him, Trust Him'; *CCH* 450, 'Father, I place into your hands'.

BIDDING PRAYERS

Ask the children if they want to pray for a sick friend, for those who care for the sick, for sick people in countries where there are no proper hospitals.

Jesus wants his followers to be generous

READING: *Listen* (Page 116) No 57B, The poor old woman. Mark 12: 41–44; Luke 21: 1–4.

One day Jesus went into the Temple and while He was there, He saw all the people putting their money into the 'poor box'. Some of the rich people put in a lot of money; but then a poor old woman came along and put in two little coins worth a penny! Jesus saw this happen and He said to his friends: 'That woman has put in more money than all the rest. For they put in the money they had to spare, but she has put in *everything* she has.'

POINTS FOR CATECHIST

Read Barclay on Mark 12: 41–44 or on Luke 21: 1–4.

This woman represents those people who in gratitude for God's gifts want to share what they have. It is important to help children recognise that all our possessions—spiritual, physical, mental, material—are gifts from God, who wants us to share them with others. Sharing brings happiness.

Jesus points out that it is not WHAT we give that counts, but the spirit in which we give. This woman is an example of a true follower of Jesus. The giving of her possessions is a sign of the giving of herself. We see the same values here as in the Incarnation; it is not what we HAVE but what we ARE that counts with God.

PRESENTATION

1. Read the passage and tell the children to try and picture the scene.

2. The 7 to 8-year-olds could act the scene and discuss the different types of people involved. See No 5.

3. Jesus noticed the people putting money in the 'poor box'.

   (a) Picture the different manner in which they might have given or act it out—some drawing attention to themselves, some throwing in thoughtlessly, some struggling with themselves on how much to give, etc.

   (b) Discuss different ways of giving:

   to show love, to be well thought of, to receive a present in return, because others are giving . . . .

   we can give time to people—helping, etc

   can put aside sweet money and have our own 'poor box'

   sharing is a form of giving—sharing a bag of sweets, sharing by helping someone with reading or spelling, sharing time by playing with someone.

4. Outwardly the woman was poor and un-important; probably ashamed at having so little to give; yet Jesus praised her. Do we judge by appearances, by what people possess (cars, houses etc), by what people can do? Do we pat ourselves on the back?

   How does Jesus judge people? To Him this woman was rich (in love, unselfish-ness, trust).

   Jesus appreciates even our smallest efforts:

   Bad at spelling but trying very hard

   Dreadful temper but great efforts to overcome it.

   With Him it is not the outward result but the *effort* which counts.

   Was Jesus rich? Did he share his gifts? DISCUSS.

5. What was going on in the mind of Jesus—the apostles—the widow—passers by—when she put her coins in the box?

ACT OF FAITH (Response: Father we thank you.)

For the greatness of your love.
For your gifts of health and strength.
For the gift of our parents.

Hymn, *CCH* No 11, 'All that I am.'

BIDDING PRAYERS (Lord Jesus, please bless them)

1. We pray for all who give to you in hidden ways.

2. We pray for those who feel ashamed at having only a little to give.

3. We pray for people who have a lot of money, that they may be generous to the poor.

AT HOME: Try to be like this woman and put aside some pocket money or ice cream money and bring it on Sunday for the poor box.

Jesus wants his followers to help each other

READING: The man who came in through the roof, *Listen* (Page 152) No 76B. Mark 2: 1-2.

When Jesus came back to Capernaum, the news got round that he was back. So many people came to listen to him, they filled the house where he was and there wasn't even space left in front of the door.

While Jesus was talking, four men came with a man on a stretcher. This man was paralysed and couldn't walk by himself, and they wanted to bring him to Jesus. There was no room for them to get in through the door. So they made a hole in the roof just over the place where Jesus was standing, and lowered the stretcher down in front of Him.

It was obvious they believed Jesus could help the man. Jesus could see that clearly, so He said: 'Stand up, my friend. Pick up your stretcher and go home.' And the man got up, picked up his stretcher at once and walked out of the house all by himself!

Everyone was astonished when they saw this, and they said: 'How good God is!'

POINTS FOR CATECHIST

Barclay's Commentary on Mark 2: 1–12.

With children leave out the passage on forgiving sins, and concentrate on the faith and perseverance of this man and his friends. Barclay describes how a hole could easily be made in the roof of an eastern house.

PRESENTATION

1. Reading.

2. What words tell us the place was crowded? Why were there so many people? Jesus drew people because He loved them; they wanted to listen to Him speaking about His Father, wanted to be healed. Cf, Mother Theresa and her nuns in Calcutta draw crowds today.

3. The man was paralysed. Discuss—unable to use his limbs— to do anything for himself—absolutely dependent on others —how would you feel? Would you long and ache for a cure? Was it the man's faith, the faith of his friends, or both, which brought them to Jesus? Where do we hear of sick people being taken today on pilgrimage? (Lourdes). Different kinds of healing take place, some physical; some given strength to live with their handicap.

4. How do these four men show they are real friends? Stand by their friend; practical help; not afraid of difficulty, or of what people would say; they *never give up*. What kind of friends are we? Do we stand by our friends in need? Forget our friends if they are ill? How do we show we care? What kind of people do we choose as friends?

5. Explain briefly how the roof could be opened up. How did the owner of the house feel?

6. Jesus was pleased with their faith and perseverance. Do we pray with faith, or do we give up and grumble when we don't get what we want? Does God sometimes say 'NO' to us if what we ask for could harm us? How do the crowd in this story differ from the nine lepers?

ACT OF FAITH from *Praise!* Page 76

Let everyone be happy   For Jesus is Lord
Let everyone be glad   For Jesus is Lord
Let everyone be full of joy   For Jesus is Lord
Or Hymn, *CCH* 353 'When I needed a neighbour'; *CCH* 352, 'Whatsoever you do'.

BIDDING PRAYERS (Lord Jesus, give them courage and strength)

1. We pray for children who are paralysed and cannot walk.

2. We pray for parents of children who are physically handicapped.

3. We pray for all teachers of the physically handicapped.

Jesus accepts us—whoever we are

READING: Jesus heals the Leper—Mark 1: 40–45, *Good News* Version.

A man suffering from a dreaded skin-disease came to Jesus, knelt down, and begged him for help. 'If you want to,' he said, 'you can make me clean.' Jesus was filled with pity, and stretched out his hand and touched him. 'I do want to,' he answered. 'Be clean!' At once the disease left the man and he was clean. Then Jesus spoke sternly to him and sent him away at once, after saying to him: 'Listen, don't tell anyone about this. But go straight to the priest and let him examine you; then in order to prove to everyone that you are cured, offer the sacrifice that Moses ordered.' But the man went away and began to spread the news everywhere.

POINTS FOR CATECHIST

Read the story, looking at it afresh. What strikes you? (Read Barclay on Mark 1: 40–45.)

Leprosy covered a variety of skin diseases. Barclay's commentary describes these. Because the disease was so dreaded and was highly contagious, anyone with a skin disorder was expelled from the community; and this at a time when they were most in need of help. As there were no doctors, if the skin complaint was healed, the person had to be declared 'clean' by the priests.

There are still lepers in the world today, suffering the same physical pain. But there are hospitals for them, and the disease can be cured if caught in time. If you can find an advert, from a paper, appealing for help for lepers or leprosy research, show it to the group.

Jesus spoke *sternly* to the leper. A strange word. Did he want to make sure the man would go to the priests first, before going amongst people? At that time this was an important rule to stop the disease spreading. The story could be dramatised.

PRESENTATION

1. Read the passage, asking children to listen carefully for what strikes them.

2. Let the children express their views.

3. Ask them if they know anything about leprosy. Explain how dreaded the disease was, how feeble the sufferers; no medicines to help—outcast from people— terrible loneliness. It is when we are sick that we need people most. Anyone with a skin disease could find themselves classed as a leper.

   The Law—lepers not allowed near people. Had to wear a bell—This man's desperation gave him courage—he was *sure* Jesus could heal him.

4. Jesus and the people—How would the apostles and the crowd around Jesus react? 'Go away' 'Jesus send him away'— might have thrown things at him out of fear. Jesus didn't reject him. What words show how Jesus felt? Read again. What did Jesus *do* to show the man he loved and accepted him?—touched him. Imagine touching a leper—Jesus could have cured him with a word but to Jesus the man was not unclean, but a person in need of healing and love. How would the apostles have felt through all this?

   Know any saint who loved lepers?—St Francis.—Fr Damien who went to nurse lepers, caught the disease and died of it.

5. What did Jesus tell the leper to do? Sent him to the priests.
   (a) This was the Law.
   (b) He must be declared 'clean' before going amongst people again. A hard law but necessary to prevent more people catching the disease and suffering.
   (c) To offer sacrifice in thanksgiving to God.

   What else did the leper do? Spread the Good News of his cure—If you are very happy and excited you want to share your happiness. Examples? Was his sharing his happiness a way of giving thanks?

6. Work still goes on for lepers today. If time, show an advertisement or ask children to look out for one.

PRESENTATION, 7–8 YEARS.

Simplify the above. Emphasise the man's need and Jesus' response. Acting the story would help the children *feel* these.

ACT OF FAITH: (Response: Alleluia!)

We believe in God the Father Almighty, who sent his Son Jesus into the World.

We believe in Jesus Christ, his only Son our Lord, who brings us healing and forgiveness.

We believe in the Holy Spirit of love who helps us become like Jesus.

Or Hymn, *CCH* 84 'Give me joy in my heart.'

BIDDING PRAYERS (Lord Jesus, please bless them.)

1. We pray, Lord, that you will give help and strength to all who suffer from leprosy.

2. We pray for all doctors and nurses who look after lepers.

3. We pray, Lord, that you will guide all those who are trying to find ways of curing this disease.

The saints are people who grow like Jesus

READING: *New World* P319. What love really means. I Cor 13: 4–7.

This is what love is like. Love is never in a hurry, and is always kindness itself. It doesn't envy anybody at all, it never boasts about itself. It's never snobbish or rude or selfish. It doesn't keep on talking about the wrong things other people do; remembering the good things is happiness enough. It's tough—it can face anything. And it never loses trust in God, or in men and women; it never loses hope; and it never gives in. Love holds good—everywhere, for everybody, for ever.

POINTS FOR CATECHIST

Wherever the word 'love' comes in the above passage, replace it with the word Jesus—and see how St Paul's description of love becomes a portrait of Jesus. The saints are people who opened themselves to God's love and so grew more and more like Jesus.

As this is the nearest Sunday to All Saints and All Souls, help the children to understand that we are all members of God's ONE family. Some of the family are already with God, others are on the way. Anyone who is in heaven is a saint but the title *Saint* is given, after their death, to those whose lives are outstanding examples to us of how we should live as Christians. Some saints are also martyrs—people who died for their faith in Jesus.

PRESENTATION

1. Ask the children to listen carefully—and see if they think this passage is a good description or portrait of Jesus.

   Reading.

2. Short discussion on the passage with reference to

   Jesus—ourselves.

3. All the members of God's family are called to be like Jesus.

   When does he call us (baptism—and daily)?

   What name is given to people belonging to God's family?

   Christians, ie other Christs.

   Where are the members of God's family?

   Some in heaven—some on their way—all round the world.

4. What do we call people who are already in heaven? Saints.
   Is it only people with the title of 'Saint' who are with God in heaven?

   Can you think of any *one* Saint and tell us something about him/her? Allow a moment's silence.

   The catechist should have one or two examples ready in case the children are slow to respond. Ask if they know anything about their name saint—if not, suggest that they try to find out.

   Discuss what makes a person a saint. Some saints were clever, some not; some were rich, some poor; Some were old, some young.

   St Joseph Benedict Labre was a beggar.

   St Bernadette had difficulty in learning and was very poor.

St Thomas Aquinas was very clever indeed.

St Elizabeth of Hungary was a Queen.

St Therese of Lisieux never left her convent but became *patron* of missionaries because she spent her life praying for them.

ACT OF FAITH (Response: We thank you, Lord Jesus.)

Make up or have the children make up a litany.

For Our Lady who looked after Jesus.
For St Joseph who taught Jesus so many things.
For St Peter who was first Pope.
For St Francis who loved God's animals.

For St Vincent de Paul who helped the poor.
For Father Damien who nursed lepers.
For St Stephen who forgave his enemies.

BIDDING PRAYERS (Lord hear us. Lord graciously hear us.)

1. Dear Jesus, we pray for Mother Theresa and her nuns who work for the poor.

2. Dear Jesus, we pray for all those who are suffering in prison because of their love for you.

3. Dear Jesus, please help us to grow more like you.

Hymn: *CCH* 409, 'Bind us together, Lord'.

Jesus wants his followers to forgive

READING: Parable of the unforgiving servant *New World* Pp90–91, 'King and Governor'. Matthew 18: 21–35.

God's way is like this. Once upon a time there was a foreign king who wanted to settle accounts with his high officers. One officer, a governor of a province, was brought to him who owed a million pounds, and he hadn't a penny left. The king ordered him to be sold—and his wife and children and whatever property he had.

The governor fell down on the ground before the king in great fear. 'Give me time,' he begged, 'and I'll pay everything back to you.' The king felt sorry for him. So he set him free, and crossed out the whole debt. The governor went off.

On the way home he met one of his fellow officers who owed him £5. He got hold of him and nearly throttled him. 'Pay me the money you owe me,' he said. His fellow officer fell down on the ground in front of him. 'Give me time,' he begged, 'and I'll pay everything back to you.' But he wouldn't listen to him; he threw him into prison, to stay there until he had paid everything back.

The other officers saw what was happening. They were very angry indeed, and they told the king everything that had happened. The king called the governor into his presence. 'You're an utter scoundrel,' he said angrily. 'I crossed out your huge debt when you begged for time to pay. Ought you not to have treated your fellow officer as I treated you, and shown him some pity?'

He handed him over to the jailors—to stay in prison until he had paid every penny back.

POINTS FOR CATECHIST

Read Barclay on Matthew 18: 21–35.

The parable highlights a theme running through Jesus' teaching: 'Blessed are the merciful, they shall obtain mercy'.

'Judge not, and you shall not be judged'; 'Forgive us our trespasses as we . . .'; and on the Cross—'Father, forgive them . . .'

The story is told in answer to Peter's question: 'Lord, if my brother keeps on sinning against me, how many times do I have to forgive him?' The emphasis is on the contrast between the two debts.

For us, nothing people do to us can compare with our failure in responding to God's love; yet he forgives us over and over again.

The parable makes a good discussion point for the 9–10 group on the meaning of sorrow and forgiveness. It is a marvellous story for dramatisation.

PRESENTATION

1. Explain that this is a *parable* told in answer to a question. Jesus is telling us a story and wants us to think out its meaning. Read the passage.

2. Discuss. What is Jesus trying to teach us? Think about the characters:

(a) What kind of a person was the king? How would you have felt in his place?

(b) How would the governor have felt at losing his wife, children, home etc? Why do you think he owed so much? What kind of a person was he?

(c) How did his fellow officers feel?

(d) Do you think the king's treatment was right? (Was the governor truly sorry? Was he being taught something?)

3. Discuss what we mean by forgiving—being forgiven.

How do we feel when we forgive—are forgiven? Is it easy to forgive?

Do we *expect* to be forgiven? What do we mean by 'being sorry'? Sorry because I upset Mummy—or because she's going to punish me? Sorry because of what people will think of me, etc? Are the words 'I'm sorry' enough? (I might be determined to get my own back!) How do we show that our sorrow is real? (trying not to do the thing again, etc).

What kind of sorrow did the governor have? Sorry because his action affected himself.

Is my sorrow sometimes like this?—Discuss.

4. When do we express sorrow to God, and ask for his forgiveness?

(a) Whenever we realise we've done something wrong.

(b) At the beginning of Mass, before going to Holy Communion, in the *Our Father* and at the sign of peace.

(c) When we go to the Sacrament of Reconciliation.

Reconciliation means making peace with. Does God always forgive us if we are sorry? (Yes.) Why do I ask for God's forgiveness if it is another person I have hurt or upset? (God loves that person and wants us to live happily and at peace.)

PRESENTATION, 7–8 YEARS

Simplify the above. Do not go into much detail. The message is that Jesus is showing us, through this story, how we should or should not behave. How, because God forgives us, we should forgive others. Let them talk about how they feel when they forgive, are forgiven. Can they give examples of how they might behave like this governor? Mum forgives me when I break her vase; I punch my sister when she breaks my toy, etc. They could act either the parable or examples of how they behave in the same way.

ACT OF FAITH

Our Father who art in heaven; Forgive us our trespasses as we forgive those who trespass against us.

Or Hymn, *CCH* 144 'It's me, It's me, It's me, O Lord'.

BIDDING PRAYERS (Lord, help them to forgive.)

1. We pray for people in countries where there is hatred and fighting.

2. We pray for families where there is argument and unhappiness.

3. We pray for people who have been unjustly treated.

Sunday before the Feast of Christ the King

READING: John 18: 37, *Jerusalem Bible*.

'You are a King then?' said Pilate. 'Yes, I am a King,' said Jesus. 'I was born for this, I came into the world for this.'

POINTS FOR CATECHIST

This session is a preparation for next Sunday's celebration. The ideas of kingdom and kinship are difficult for children in the modern world. The emphasis should be on the joy of belonging to Jesus' kingdom.

His kingdom is universal. It is within the hearts of all those who accept Jesus and want to love and serve him. It is for all people and is not bounded by space or time. Jesus came in order to establish the Kingdom of his Father; a kingdom of love, joy, peace, forgiveness; a kingdom in which God's rule would be supreme. He did this *not* by political means but by LOVE. His was an authority of service.

Next week the children will be celebrating all that they have learnt during the term. The notes for the previous Sundays should be read through briefly, therefore. It is also essential to read next Sunday's celebration.

PRESENTATION

1. Gospel reading.

2. What kind of person do the children think of when they hear the word 'king'? What kind of a king was Jesus? Is he still King? Where is his kingdom? Who belongs to it? What was his crown like?

   What does Jesus want of his followers?

   Refer back to what they have learnt this term: he wants us to trust him, to forgive, to care for each other, etc. How can we help to spread his kingdom?

3. Prepare the children for next Sunday's celebration. Read through the hymn (*CCH* 43) and explain what is going to happen next Sunday.

   Why do they think this hymn has been chosen?

   Choose 3 or 4 Readers and one child to be Jesus. Group the rest of the children for the 5 verses. Practise with verse 1, the chorus, and the last verse.

   The readers should practise during the week, and 'Jesus' should read through the hymn at home and think about his miming.

ACT OF FAITH

Pause to reflect on one thing I can do each day this week in honour of Jesus, my King.

> Prayer: Our Father, thy kingdom come; thy will be done.
> Hymn: Chorus of 'Christ is our King'.

AT HOME

Make a banner in honour of Jesus your King *and bring it next Sunday*. It will be pinned up on the wall.

Suggestions for banner: 'Jesus is my King'; 'We belong to Jesus'; 'Hail, Christ our King'; 'King of Peace'.

Or Decorate a Cross or the letters 'IHS' ...

Celebration for Christ the King

REQUIRED: Large Christ Candle; wall sheet with chorus and last verse of Hymn 43, *CCH*, hymn books for Readers; children's banners to be pinned up.

AIM: of the Celebration—to touch our hearts so that we *feel* joyful in having Jesus as our King; and to gather together in celebration all that we have been learning this term.

The celebration

LEADER: Explain that we are celebrating a great feast. We think about all that we have learnt this term; the kind of person Jesus is, what he wants of us. We celebrate our thanks to him for calling us to be his followers, and we pray for his kingdom to spread throughout the world. The large candle stands for Jesus our King who is the Light of the World.

Remind the children of what is going to happen during the celebration. Place them in five groups, according to the five verses, with the readers and 'Jesus' at the side. Give some ideas on how to mime the different parts.

Leader (or a child) holds up the Christ candle and says: 'Hail, Christ our King!'

All repeat: 'Hail, Christ our King!'

All sing the chorus of Hymn 43.

Readers, verse 1. The 'blind' group join in with the last line, 'He is the Light of the world'. During the reading 'Jesus' moves round the group, touching the eyes of each one. They respond in mime.

All sing the chorus when the miming has finished.

Readers, verse 2. The 'poor' join in with the last line. 'Jesus' speaks to each one in mime. They respond.

All sing the chorus.

Readers, verse 3. The 'imprisoned' join in with the last line. 'Jesus' mimes bringing them freedom. They respond.

All, sing the chorus.

Readers, verse 4. The 'dumb' join in with the last line. 'Jesus' touches the lips of each one and they respond in mime.

All sing the chorus.

Readers, verse 5. The 'crippled' join in with the last line. 'Jesus' mimes the healing of each one and they respond.

All sing the chorus.

All read the last verse from the wall sheet. 'Jesus' moves to the front with the Christ candle. The last line is said more loudly with the children either kneeling or standing while stretching out their arms towards 'Jesus'.

As the chorus starts, Jesus leads everyone dancing round the altar, swaying and clapping hands in joy. He leads them into the procession back to church and offers the candle to the priest.

OR

If there is still time to go after the singing of the chorus, the children stand round the altar. 'Jesus' places the candle on the altar and the Leader continues:

Leader: We now pray the special prayer which Jesus our King has given to us. We look at the candle flame and pray that just as this flame spreads its light, so the light of Jesus may spread throughout the world until all people belong to his Kingdom. We hold hands as we pray. This is a sign that we BELONG to each other and to Jesus.

OUR FATHER

We end with the special sign we have to show that we belong to Jesus.

SIGN OF THE CROSS

Jesus takes the candle from the altar and leads the procession back into church. During the procession the chorus may be sung.

Notes for Advent

OUR AIM: To put Christ into Christmas.

1. In telling the Christmas story we must be aware of the central message: We know about God's loving care for us because Jesus has come into our world, into our lives.

   The Incarnation is not just about something that happened two thousand years ago. *IT IS TAKING PLACE NOW.*

   The Incarnation is a quite unique event in the history of the world. The explosion of God into our world has far greater consequences than any nuclear explosion, however great. The world will never be the same again.

2. Our own attitudes are all important. What does Christmas mean to *me*?

   What is my attitude in sending Christmas cards, giving presents etc?

   Am I trying to bring God's love to the world through all the hustle and bustle? What do I *mean* when I say: 'Happy Christmas'?

   These are important questions we need to ask ourselves.

3. In our presentation we make use of all the external, secular Christmas preparations —in shops, schools, at home; the sending of cards, buying presents, putting up decorations, etc—to heighten the idea of CELEBRATION and then to help children understand that we are celebrating God's love made present in Jesus.

4. We use religious symbols to put across the message of the Gospel writers: *this birth is unique*; the advent wreath, making of cribs, carols, stars, lights, etc.

5. We help the children to understand that it is Christ's birthday we are celebrating. He is not born again. In celebrating the birthday of Him who came to spread love, happiness and peace, we have to be aware of others: our own family, our friends, the lonely, the poor. ALL are our brothers and sisters.

6. For ourselves as adults, we should be aware that we are celebrating the three comings of Jesus: His coming in the past; His coming today; His coming in the future.

7. NB, the readings from Isaiah are suitable for choral reading by the children, and could be printed on card and hung up. The same could be done for the prayer to be said with the Advent Wreath, and for the words of the hymn.

   When the scripture readings are from the Old Testament we use the response: This is the Word of the Lord: Thanks be to God. Help the children to make the response a real act of thanksgiving.

THE ADVENT WREATH

This is an old German custom. It is a reminder that we are preparing to celebrate the coming of Jesus, the Light of the World.

There are four candles, one for each Sunday of Advent. During the first week of Advent we light one candle, during the second week two candles, etc. The light on our wreath becomes stronger, the nearer we get to Christmas.

The symbolism

Circle: Jesus comes to bring everlasting life (unending circle). *Evergreens* are little affected by changing seasons and symbolise God's unchanging love which Jesus brings to us. *Candles* symbolise Jesus, the Light of the World. The date chosen for Christmas is near to the winter solstice, when the world is in darkness and the days are beginning to grow lighter again.

Many families have their own Advent wreath and gather in front of it for prayer each evening.

Hymns and Carols for use with the wreath.

The world was in darkness
And nobody knew
The way to the Father
as you and I do.
They needed a light
that would show them the way;
And the great light shone
On Christmas Day.

OR

Christmas time is coming,
It's getting very near.
We've only (4) more weeks to wait
To greet you, Jesus dear.
We have lit(one) candle,
to shine here bright and gay
For Jesus will bring happiness with him on
    Christmas Day.

Question-and-answer carol (said or sung in dialogue)

Why are there lights on the Christmas tree?
    Jesus the Lord lights the world for me.
Why are there grand things to eat instead?
    Jesus the Lord is the Living Bread.
Why are there presents for everyone?
    God gave us Jesus, his dearest Son.

Why are there carols for us to sing?
    Jesus the Lord is our mighty King.
Why are there crackers, and games, and mirth?
    Jesus the Lord has brought joy to earth.
What is the bet gift that God has given?
    Jesus the Lord to lead us to heaven.

[*MUSIC: PAGE 72*]

Advent 1: Light

READING: Isaiah 9: 2, *Good News* version.

The people who walked in darkness
    have seen a great light.
They lived in a land of shadows,
    but now a light is shining on them.
You have given them great joy, Lord;
    you have made them very happy.
They rejoice in what you have done.

POINTS FOR CATECHIST

Read the general notes for Advent.

Our aim is to help the children understand that Christmas is the celebration of the birthday of Jesus, the Light of the World.

Light comes to us so easily from the electricity company that we need to think about its symbolism: it is necessary for life and growth; it guides, comforts, beautifies; it penetrates the darkest corners and *always* overcomes darkness.

Because of the necessity of light for life, men have always equated darkness with evil, light with salvation. Around the 3rd century AD the Romans instituted the Feast of the Unconquerable Sun. December 25th was chosen, being a time when the sun, which seemed to have sunk beneath the powers of darkness, began to rise again. The Christian Church took over the feast and put new meaning into it, celebrating the coming into the world of the *true* unconquerable sun, Jesus Christ. Light is a powerful symbol for children, helping them to understand the greatness of Jesus.

PRESENTATION

1. *Reading*. This can be read by the catechist or in groups. Explain that the prophet Isaiah who wrote it lived a long time before Jesus. He is describing how God came to the rescue when people had lost their way in selfishness and sin. He does the same for us, and sends his Son to be our Guide.

2. *7–8 years*. Ask the children how they feel about darkness and light: walking down a lane in the dark and feeling lost; bewildered and groping for things during a power cut; unable to watch TV or to read, etc, during a power cut; how they feel on a dismal / bright day. Jesus said: 'I am the Light of the World'. What did he mean?

3. *9–10 years*.
   (a) Discuss the different things light does for us: necessary for life and growth; guides us—lightships, cats' eyes on roads, car lights, torches; gives us power—penetrates darkest places, conquers darkness; beautifies—no colour without light; comforts, etc.

   (b) Light can have other meanings for us: 'Oh, I see what you mean.' 'I don't see it that way.' 'I still feel in the dark.' 'Can you throw any light on this?'

   (c) Jesus said: 'I am the Light of the World'. What did he mean? Refer back to the reading from Isaiah and let them say what *they* think it means.

4. *All ages*. Have you ever thought of why shops are full of candles before Christmas—all shapes, sizes, colours?

   Try to draw out the idea that candles remind us of Jesus, our Light.

Ask the children if they think people realise this.

Suggest that they have either a Christmas candle or Advent wreath in their living room or bedroom and light it carefully each evening for prayer as a reminder that Jesus was sent by God to light up the world.

ACT OF FAITH

Ask them why we have the Advent wreath made (a) in a circle, (b) with evergreens, (c) with four candles.
   Light ONE candle.
   Read or get the children to read the passage from Isaiah.
   Allow a minute for silent prayer.
   Prayer together: Come Lord Jesus, be a light for us.
   Hymn: 'The world was in darkness ...'; or 'Christmas time is coming'; or *CCH* 536, 'Light the Advent Candle' (v1).

Advent 2: Preparation

READING: Luke 3: 4–6 quoted from Isaiah 40: 3–5, *Good News* version.

Someone is shouting in the desert:
   'Get the road ready for the Lord;
make a straight path for him to travel!
   Every valley must be filled up,
every hill and mountain levelled off.
   The winding roads must be made straight,
and the rough paths made smooth.
   All mankind will see God's salvation!'

POINTS FOR CATECHIST

Read general notes for Advent.
   Our aim is to arouse in the children a sense of expectancy and longing and a desire to prepare their hearts for Jesus' birthday.
   The reading speaks of preparing. It is quite difficult but has the right note of expectancy and joy. If written on card and hung up, it could be said by the children.
   Before Jesus came, people knew something about God, but their ideas were distorted; they had lost their way. And so God sent his Son to light up the way, to show people how to live. See last week's notes. Advent (from *Advenio*— I come) is a time of waiting, of preparation for the Coming One.

The Advent wreath and Advent tree are two ways of helping children to keep their eyes on the true meaning of Christmas amid the bustle of external preparations.

PRESENTATION

1. Gospel Reading. Explain that it is from the same prophet Isaiah of last week's reading.

2. *Preparing*. Draw from the children the various occasions we prepare for in life: birthdays, weddings, a new baby, bazaars, moving house, a visit. . . .

   Sometimes we prepare on our own, sometimes together. The bigger the event, the greater the preparation.

   Ask one or two children to describe how they prepared for some event, and how they felt in preparing. Was the event worth all the effort?

   What are shops preparing for now? How are they preparing?

3. *Advent preparation*. Explain the word Advent. For what are *we* preparing? Why do we need to prepare? How can we prepare?

Mary is our example. She did not remain idle. All her thoughts were on her coming baby.

How would she have prepared? Getting ready the things needed—praying for help in this great task. . . .

She also found time to go and help her cousin.

Each evening at home we can ask Mary to help us prepare for her Son's birthday.

4. One way of keeping our thoughts on the real meaning of Christmas is to make an *Advent tree.* We can make it as a family.

(a) either draw a tree on a long sheet of paper—wallpaper will do—or find a branch of a tree and place it in a pot.

(b) Count the days until Christmas and make one symbol for each day. Each evening, with your family if possible, hang or stick one symbol on your Advent Tree. Sing the verse of a hymn or carol and pray: 'COME, LORD JESUS!'

Ideas for symbols may come to mind after each Sunday's session. The following are some suggestions:

Decorated M for Mary;

tools for Joseph;
a donkey, an inn door;
a shepherd's crook, a lamb;
a manger, star, angel,
gold crown, incense boat, box of myrrh;
candle for Jesus our light;
loaf of bread for Jesus the Bread of Life;
IHS for Jesus Saviour of Men;
a fish, secret symbol for Jesus in early Church;
an olive twig—sign of the peace Jesus brings;
two hands grasped in handshake—sign of reconciliation;
yourself—your family;
a BABY for December 25th.

ACT OF FAITH

Light TWO candles on the Advent wreath.

The passage from Isaiah read by catechist or by the children.

Allow a minute for silent prayer asking Mary to help us prepare our hearts.

Prayer: Dear Mary, please help everyone in this parish to prepare their hearts for the birthday of your Son.

Hymn: 'The World was in darkness' or 'Christmas time is coming'; or *CCH* 536 (v2).

Advent 3: The message

READING: Luke 2: 4–19, *Good News* version adapted.

Joseph went from the town of Nazareth in Galilee to the town of Bethlehem in Judaea, the birthplace of King David. He went there because he was a descendant of David. He went to register with Mary, his wife, who was about to have a baby.

While they were there, her baby was born. He was a boy and she wrapped him in strips of cloth, or swaddling clothes, and laid him in a manger—because there was no room for them to stay in the inn.

In the countryside close by there were shepherds who lived in the fields and took it in turns to watch their flocks during the night. The angel of the Lord appeared to them and the glory of the Lord shone round them. They were terrified, but the angel said: 'Don't be afraid. Listen, I am here with good news for you,

which will bring great joy to all the people. This very day in David's town your Saviour was born; He is Christ the Lord. And here is a SIGN for you: you will find a baby wrapped in swaddling clothes and lying in a manger.'

Suddenly with the angel there was a great throng of angels, praising God and singing: 'Glory to God in the highest, and peace to his people on earth.'

When the angels went back into heaven, the shepherds said to one another: 'Let's go to Bethlehem and see this thing that has happened, which the Lord has told us about.' So they hurried off, and found Mary and Joseph; and they saw the baby lying in the manger.

When the shepherds saw the child, they repeated what the angels had told them about him. And everyone who heard it was astonished. As for Mary, she treasured all these things and thought deeply about them.

The shepherds went back singing praises to God for all they had heard and seen.

POINTS FOR CATECHIST

Read the general notes for Advent.

Our aim is to help the children to a deeper understanding of the Christmas story.

All through the ages God was calling his people to a deeper understanding of Himself; of what he wanted of them, and for them. He sent *prophets*, men who proclaimed his message; but people often misunderstood the message and rejected the messengers. Finally God sent his own Son.

Jesus is the message. He, himself, is the Good News. St John writes: 'The Word became human... Nobody has ever seen God himself. The Beloved Son who knows the Father's thoughts has made him plain.'

Read this account of the Nativity and ponder the message it holds for *you*. St Luke is writing after the Resurrection and is concerned less with the story than with explaining the message of who Jesus is for us; and of *what happened when he entered our world*. We see our values turned upside down.

One way of helping children to disentangle the original story from the legends which have grown up around it is to take the Nativity scene and let them find the message within it.

PRESENTATION

1. Briefly recall that Advent is a time of preparation. Do any of them remember what the word means? When God sent his Son to earth many people didn't recognise him because they weren't prepared. Are we remembering to prepare? What are we doing?

2. *Gospel Reading*—tell the children to listen carefully. Pictures often add to the story. We want to hear what the *writer* tells us. Picture the scene as *he* describes it.

3. God has a special message for us in this story. Let each one say *one* thing which struck them as the story was being read. Now we will try to discover God's message—use the children's suggestions. The following are likely to be mentioned: A baby—why did God send his Son as a baby? What is he trying to tell us? A mother—why did he need a mother? What kind of a person was she? Joseph—was he rich, important...? A stable—a manger—what do these tell us? Angels—in scripture they are always a SIGN of God's presence. Shepherds—poor and despised.

Does the writer mention the ox and ass? Why do we have them pictured? Does God think like us? Would we have chosen to come like this if we wanted to save the world? How would you have chosen to come? Would you have been right?

4. *9–10 years, at home*: Design two Christmas cards—one missing the whole point of Christmas, one showing the message and meaning of Christmas.

If the catechist of the 7–8 group thinks the children capable of doing this, then it can be suggested to them as well.

Bring the two cards next week.

ACT OF FAITH

Light THREE candles on the Advent wreath.

Reading: 'Here is a sign for you; you will find a baby wrapped in swaddling clothes and lying in a manger.'

Allow a minute for silent prayer.

Prayer: Dear God our Father, we thank you for sending your Son Jesus to us as a baby, so that we won't be afraid of him. Please help us to love him. Amen.

Hymn: 'The world was in darkness ...' or 'Christmas time is coming'; or *CCH* 536 (v3).

Advent 4: Presents

READING: Isaiah 9: 6. *Good News* version.

A Child is born to us!
A Son is given to us!
And he will be our ruler
He will be called, 'Wonderful Counsellor,
  Mighty God,
Eternal Father, PRINCE OF PEACE'.

POINTS FOR CATECHIST

Read the general notes for Advent, as well as the notes for the previous Sundays.

Our aim is to help the children understand Christmas as the celebration of God's greatest gift to mankind.

A person who accepts life and all that it holds as a gift from God is a happy person. Our God is a giver of gifts, and mankind is a gifted race. Appreciation of this will give children a sense of gratitude; and grateful people are happy people.

Are we, ourselves, aware of all that we receive; are we grateful to God?

God communicates with us, reveals himself to us, through his gifts. The greatest *revelation* and *gift* is his Son Jesus.

PRESENTATION

1. Ask to see the two cards the children designed at home. The 7–8 group may not have done them.

2. Read the passage and explain that it is from the same prophet as the earlier readings.

3. Ask the children why we give presents; what is a present saying?

   Presents are a way of celebrating. When we celebrate a birthday we are celebrating our love for the person. Love is always there but we highlight it, remind ourselves of it.

   How do we choose presents? Does the *way* we choose, say something about us?

   Do we try to disguise our present? Why? Which is more important, the wrapping or the present?

   Do we show our thanks by the way we treat presents given to us?

4. Do we realise God is giving us gifts all the time as signs of his love? Discuss these gifts, getting ideas from the children. Gifts of creation, our senses, mental gifts, our parents and family, friends, the Church, the sacraments, etc.

   How do we treat these gifts of God?

5. During Advent we are preparing to receive God's greatest gift to us: His Son Jesus.

   Listen to the reading again.

Why did God send Jesus to us? Was God's gift wrapped up?

Would you have recognised the baby in the manger as this Mighty God and Prince of Peace?

God still comes in hidden ways. Can you think of any? In Holy Communion; in people; in events.

Do we recognise him?

NB, this is a difficult concept. The younger group will probably only cope with the idea of God coming hidden in Communion.

6. In celebrating Jesus' birthday we are reminding ourselves of God's greatest gift to us.

   Why do we give gifts to *each other* when it is Jesus' birthday we celebrate? To spread the same happiness that Jesus came to bring. Jesus takes as done to himself what we do for others.

   What else can we do to spread love and happiness this Christmas? Send Christmas cards; decorate our homes; be helpful; visit someone lonely; have someone to stay or to share our Christmas dinner; give some of *our own* money to the poor.

   Jesus comes as Prince of Peace. We can go to the Sacrament of Reconciliation and ask God to forgive us for the times we have upset peace at home or in school, and ask him to help us be peaceful people during the Christmas holiday.

ACT OF FAITH

Light ALL four candles on the Advent wreath.

Read the passage or get the children to read it together.

Allow a minute for silent prayer.

Prayer: Dear God, our Father, we thank you for the gift of your Son, Jesus. Please help us to spread his happiness in the world. Amen.

Hymn: 'The world was in darkness ...' or 'Christmas time is coming'; or *CCH* 536 (v4).

Notes for Sundays after Christmas

In this scheme we see how Jesus came for *all* people.

At his baptism he was consecrated to the service of his Father; to the work of establishing and spreading God's Kingdom on earth.

At our baptism we also are consecrated to the service of God, our Father; a service of *prayer* and *action*.

1. The Wise Men Come to Jesus.
   Jesus comes for *all* people.

2. The Baptism of Jesus—a celebration.

His consecration to his Father.

3. We live our baptism by trying to live like Jesus.
   The importance of *actions* and not just words.

4. The *Our Father*—session one.

5. The *Our Father*—session two.

6. The *Our Father*—session three.
   The importance of *prayer* in the Christian life.

The Wise Men come to Jesus

READING: *Listen* (Pages 52 and 53) No 24 adapted. Matthew 2: 1–12.

When Jesus was born in Bethlehem he received a visit from some Wise Men.

First they came to Jerusalem, and they said to King Herod: 'Where will we find the baby who is the King of the Jews? For we have seen his star in the East and we have come to worship him.'

King Herod didn't like this. (He didn't want anyone to be king except himself!) But he asked the priests and the teachers if they knew anything about it, and they said: 'A long time ago God spoke to the people of Bethlehem like this: "I promise you, the Great King will be born in Bethlehem. He will look after you like a shepherd who looks after his sheep. He will take care of you. He will never let you down, for he will be the King of the World!".'

So King Herod sent his visitors off to Bethlehem. 'You find the baby,' he said. 'Then come back and tell me where I can find him, and I will go and see him as well.'

So the Wise men went to Bethlehem, and they found Jesus there with his mother, Mary,

and kneeling down, they gave him their presents of gold, frankincense, and myrrh.

But they didn't trust King Herod, and they didn't go back to him.

POINTS FOR CATECHIST

The word 'Epiphany' means manifestation or showing forth. This reading is used on the Sunday nearest to the Feast of the Epiphany.

In calling the shepherds (Jews), the Wise Men (Gentiles), God shows that Jesus has come to save *all* people. Jesus says of Himself: 'I am the Light of *the world*' and 'I am the Way'. This star symbolises Jesus, Our Light, who has come to guide us to the Father. It is with the eyes of faith that we recognise him.

There has been much controversy over the 'star'. It is impossible to identify a particular heavenly body as the star of Bethlehem. Although the allusion is not explicit, the Jewish reader would recognise the star that rises from Jacob in the Book of Numbers, chapter 24 v 17. And Matthew was writing for Jewish Christians.

Matthew is telling us that it was to a waiting

world that Jesus came, and when he came the ends of the world were gathered at his cradle. This is the first sign and symbol of the world conquest of Christ.

The gifts symbolise: gold—kingship; frankincense—priesthood; myrrh—death.

Nowhere are we told that these men were kings; nor are we told that there were three. This has become tradition. We do not know where they came from.

Certainly at the time of the Incarnation men were waiting expectantly for some sign from God. Magi were originally learned Persian priests; later it meant anyone learned in the occult and in astrology.

PRESENTATION

1. Gospel reading.
2. Let the children say what they like most about the story.

   What do *they* think it is telling us?

3. Some important points:

   Jesus comes for everybody: the poor and unlearned—shepherds; the rich and wise—wise men.

   How do we know they were wise and rich?

   How did God show these men the way to the Saviour? How did they know what the star meant?

   God shows us the way. How? (Through parents, priests, teachers, our conscience.)

4. The Wise Men followed God's call in trust and so found Jesus. Was it easy for them to leave their families and homes on this long, hard, uncertain journey? Would their families have understood? Or would they have laughed and jeered? What would Mum think if Dad suddenly said he'd seen a comet and must follow it? Did they know where their journey would end?

   Do we find it hard to do what God wants? Are we sometimes laughed at, or do we laugh at others for doing right?

5. They knelt to this poor baby. Why? Why did they give him presents?

   Do you think it was easy for them to recognise the Son of God in this poor, helpless baby?

ACT OF FAITH

'We three Kings' or some suitable carol.

BIDDING PRAYERS (Lord, hear us we pray)

1. Dear God, please help those who have power to use it wisely.

2. Dear God, please help us to follow our star each day.

3. Dear God, please help us to understand that Jesus came for us all, and wants us to love each other.

The Baptism of Jesus: A celebration

Needed: Christ Candle; small candles; responses on large card; Pictures of Jesus' baptism and of a baby being baptised; Cards with 'Love'—'Joy'—'Peace'—'Forgiveness' for pinning up. Focus cards on God's Family or pictures from colour magazines of family scenes. Words of the chorus to 'Lord of the Dance'. Copy of *Listen*. Two tapers.

POINTS FOR CATECHIST

This celebration aims at helping children understand that baptism is not just something which happened in the past. We *are* baptised, and as we grow up we have to live out our baptism daily. A birthday celebration *highlights* our love for someone; the love is always there.

Today's celebration makes us stop and think—how glad we are to be God's children. How can we make our response to his love?

CELEBRATION

1. Refer to the pictures of Jesus' baptism and the baby's baptism. Jesus was consecrated, set aside for the service of his Father. It is the same with the baby. What does the priest *do* and *say* when he baptises?

2. Use the Focus cards or magazine pictures to draw from the children what it means to *belong* to a family. Baptism is a sacrament of belonging.

3. When Jesus was baptised he promised to do all his Father wanted him to do. He promised to found God's kingdom, the Church, made up of people who would try to spread God's message of love, joy, peace, forgiveness. Do the children remember the celebration they had on the Feast of Christ the King? (The catechist may need to look this up beforehand.)

4. When we were baptised our parents asked the priest to receive us into God's family, the Church, and they promised to help us live as his children. Just as a baby is welcomed with great joy by its family, so all the people in church welcomed us when we were baptised. Some of you will remember a baptism at Sunday Mass. When the priest poured the water and said the words, we received that life of Jesus which makes us members of God's family.

As we grow older and can think for ourselves, we want to tell God, our Father, we are glad to be his children and we will try to live in his way. In this celebration we come together to thank God for his love, to tell him we believe in him, and to ask for his help to live as his children.

5. The Christ Candle on the altar stands for Jesus. When we were baptised, the priest prayed: 'Receive the light of Christ—walk always as a child of the light.'

   Our candles will be lit from the Christ Candle; then together we will renew our baptismal promises. The responses are on the card.

   Our responses should be *joyful* and the 'Alleluia' reminds us of this.

   Does anyone remember what this word means?

   Have two children ready with tapers.

   The story of Jesus' baptism may be read if desired and time allows: *Listen* No 27.

Leader: Receive the Light of Christ

Two children with tapers light them, stand each side of the altar, and the other children come forward to have their candles lit. They then return to their places.
When everyone is in place:

Leader: Do you believe that God is your loving Father?

All: Yes, I believe that God is my loving Father. Alleluia!

Leader: Are you glad that you are a child of God?

All: Yes, I am glad that I am a child of God. Alleluia!

Leader: Do you want to follow Jesus?

All: Yes, I want to follow Jesus. Alleluia!

Leader: Do you ask Jesus for the help of his Spirit?

All: Yes, I ask Jesus for the help of his Spirit. Alleluia!

Leader: Do you thank God for all his love and care?

All: Yes, I thank God for all his love and care. Alleluia!

Leader: We now pray the special prayer of God's family, asking that Jesus' Kingdom of love, joy, peace, and forgiveness may spread throughout the world. While praying, we look at our candle flame. The flame spreads light in the darkness, and our prayers can bring God's light and love to people who don't know him.

Our Father

Blow out candles. Collect them.

Our lives are like a dance with joyful and sad moments, we dance along following Jesus our Leader. And so we finish our celebration with the *chorus* of 'Lord of the Dance' (sung twice). We hold hands and dance joyfully into a line for the procession of the Gifts. The labels and pictures can be given out and carried in procession to the altar.

Chorus to 'Lord of the Dance'.

> Dance then, wherever you may be
>   I am the Lord of the Dance, said he.
> And I'll lead you all
>   Wherever you may be.
> And I'll lead you all
>   In the dance, said he.

CCH 614, 'The light of Christ'.

We live our Baptism by trying to live like Jesus

READING: Helping the least of my brothers, *New World* P100.) Matthew 25: 31–45.

Jesus said:
>   I was hungry and you gave me food;
>   I was thirsty and you gave me drink;
>   I was a foreigner and you took me home with you;
>   I was in rags and you gave me clothes;
>   I fell ill and you looked after me;
>   I was in prison and you came to see me.
> Believe me—
>   when you helped the least of my brothers, you helped me.
>
>   I was hungry and you gave me no food;
>   I was thirsty and you gave me no drink;
>   I was a foreigner and you didn't take me home with you;
>   I was in rags and you gave me no clothes;
>   I fell ill and you didn't look after me;
>   I was in prison and you never came to see me.
> Believe me—
>   when you didn't help the least of my brothers,
>   you didn't help me.

POINTS FOR CATECHIST

Ponder this parable: what does it say to *you*? (Barclay: Matthew: 25: 31–45.)

The message of the parable is that God judges us not on how much we know, how famous we are, or on our great deeds. He judges us on how we *notice* human needs and respond to them. We are not asked to give vast sums of money, but to help in simple, ordinary ways. The people who help are uncalculating; they do not help in order to win approval; they expect no return and are surprised when they are praised.

Generosity without calculation brings its own blessing and happiness.

PRESENTATION, 9–10 YEARS

1. Explain that this is a parable. Listen for its hidden meaning.

2. Gospel Reading.

3. What is Jesus trying to teach us in the parable?
   Can children:
   (a) Visit people in prison?

   Are there ways of being imprisoned other than being behind bars?

   Do loneliness, sickness, sadness, physical or mental disability imprison people?

Are there people living near us who are imprisoned in any of these ways?

(b) Give food and drink to the hungry and thirsty? How?

(c) Take a 'foreigner' home with them? Who might be termed a foreigner?

(d) clothe someone or look after someone who is ill?

4. What kind of needs do we meet? How does Jesus want us to respond?

Dad comes in worn out—
Mum has a heavy load of shopping—
Jim is in bed with measles—
Our baby is crying—
Granny is in hospital—
Sheila is new to our class and gets left out—
Our parish gives help to an Indian parish—
There is a severely disabled spastic living near us—

WHAT CAN I DO?

5. When we help, are we calculating? Do we want to be noticed?

Do we only help when we are sure of being noticed?

Do we expect to be paid for helping? Was Jesus paid for helping people?

In a sense Jesus was paid—by the happiness of the people he helped. This can be true for us also.

6. 'If you tried to help someone, you did something for me.'

Do we ever think of this when we help someone?

PRESENTATION, 7–8 YEARS (simplify the above)

1. Jesus asks us to help people. In what ways can we help?

Let each child give an example of how they help others. They could act or mime it.

2. When we do things for others, we make Jesus happy. Do we make ourselves happy also?

ACT OF FAITH

CCH 352, v 1 'Whatsoever you do'; *AK* 73, and *CCH* 320 The Beatitudes.

BIDDING PRAYERS (Lord Jesus, please bless and help them)

1. We pray for our Mummies and Daddies who take such care of us.

2. Do you know anyone who is lonely that you would like to pray for?

3. Do you know anyone who is sick or disabled that you would like to pray for?

4. Lord, we pray for people who are imprisonned in any way.

SOMETHING TO DO

This week I will try to help someone each day without being asked.

Jesus teaches his followers to pray

This theme on the 'Our Father' covers three Sundays

Jesus teaches the Our Father in answer to the Disciples' request: 'Lord, teach us to pray.'

The Jews were a praying people and so there must have been a special quality about the prayer of Jesus which led them to make this request. It is the most important of all Christian prayers, given us by Jesus himself. Jesus is really giving us a pattern for all our prayer. He places it in the context of the family of God. He puts God's glory first, and only after that the needs of people. Is this how we pray?

Jesus prayed in Aramaic; we have a *translation*, and so there are different versions of the prayer in English. Also, the Gospels of Matthew and Luke have slight variations in their texts showing that there were two traditions of the Lord's prayer in the early Church.

Use the normal text of the prayer for the 7–8 group. For the older group, one of the other texts can be used; or two different texts can be used, showing the differences.

MATTHEW (*Jerusalem Bible* Ch 6 v 9)

Our Father in heaven,
may your name be held holy,
your kingdom come,
your will be done,
on earth as in heaven.
Give us today our daily bread.
And forgive us our debts,
as we have forgiven those who are in debt to
    us.
And do not put us to the test,
but save us from the evil one.

LUKE (*Jerusalem Bible* Ch 11 v 2)

Father, may your name be held holy,
your kingdom come,
give us each day our daily bread,
and forgive us our sins,
for we ourselves forgive each one who is in
    debt to us.
And do not put us to the test.

Barclay: Matthew 6: 9–15; Luke 11: 2–4.

These notes contain a great deal of material. It might be best to spend the main part of each session on one petition, just referring to the others. Those taking these sessions on the *Our Father* should read the notes for all three Sundays.

'Our Father': Session One

POINTS FOR CATECHIST

Read the general notes on the *Our Father*.

PRESENTATION

1. *Gospel Reading:*
   Jesus said to his friends: 'When you pray don't make a lot of fuss so that everyone looks at you. Find somewhere where you can be quiet. Then talk to God, our Father, like this:

   > Our Father who art in heaven... Say the whole prayer slowly and prayerfully.

   9–10 years: If you wish, read the shorter version of the prayer and explain that there have always been two versions. It was passed down by word of mouth for years before it was written down. It is essentially the same prayer.

2. His disciples asked Jesus to teach them to pray. He gave them this prayer as a pattern for all their prayers. Notice how he starts with God and His glory before mentioning people's needs.

   Is this how we pray? Or do we start by asking for things?

   Do we remember to praise God and to thank him for all his gifts and for being our Father?

Sometimes we can pray just a phrase at a time:

> Our Father, thy will be done.
> Our Father, forgive us our trespasses...

Over the next two Sundays we are going to think about this prayer.

3. *Our Father*: Ask for comments:
   (a) Father—what does this tell us about God?
   (b) 'our'—not 'my', because this is the prayer of God's family. He is Father of *all* people, *everywhere*. Discuss the kinds of people in God's family: rich—poor; healthy—sick; old—young; good—bad; etc.

   9–10 years: In praying these words we are accepting that we belong to the family of God. What does this mean for us? Do we accept and treat people as our brothers and sisters:—those we like, those we don't like; those who live near, those who live far away? If all Christians *lived* what they *prayed*, would the world be a happier place?

   7–8 years: When I see people at school—on the bus—in shops—people I like, people I don't like I will stop and think: God is *your* Father; God is *their* Father; God is *our* Father; and I will pray for them.

4. *In heaven*: What do we mean when we say God is in Heaven? Where is Heaven?

   God is not confined to one place. We can pray to him anywhere at any time.

   Heaven is where God is. It is his home.

   > When I'm very happy;
   > When I've just received Jesus in Communion;
   > When I'm close to God in prayer;
   > When I've just received God's forgiveness in the Sacrament or from another person...

   then I have some idea of Heaven, of being with God, my Father.

ACT OF FAITH

Our Father, who art in heaven... we love you.

Our Father, who art in heaven... we trust you.

Our Father, who art in heaven... we thank you for being a father to us.

BIDDING PRAYERS (Response: Father in heaven, help us)

1. Our Father, please help us to remember to pray to you.

2. Our Father, please help us to remember that all people are your children.

3. Our Father, please help us to be grateful for your gifts.

AT HOME

Each evening this week with your family or on your own reflect on the words: 'Our Father, who art in heaven ...' and say them as your night prayer.

'Our Father': Session Two

POINTS FOR CATECHIST

Read the general notes for the *Our Father*.

PRESENTATION

1. Refer briefly to last week.

2. *Gospel Reading*: say slowy and prayerfully: Our Father, who art in heaven, Hallowed be thy Name. Thy Kingdom come, thy will be done on earth as it is in heaven.

3. *Hallowed be thy Name*: What do the children think this means?

   'Hallowed', ie, reverenced, held holy, praised, glorified.

   Name: A name stands for the person. In glorifying God's name, we are glorifying God. What are the things that show forth God's glory?—His power, his beauty, his love... Get suggestions from the children: Beauty of creation—first words of a baby—love of parents—gifts of mind and body—courage of the disabled—wonders of technology which are possible because of God's gift of intellect—marvels of medical research, etc.

   Discuss how *we* can glorify God's name: recognising his gifts and using them, caring for his creation.

   Which prayer at Mass speaks of God's glory? 'Holy, holy, holy...'

4. *Thy Kingdom come, thy will be done.*
   The second phrase explains how God's Kingdom will come. What are we asking in this petition? What is a kingdom? Is God's Kingdom bounded by frontiers? No—it is for *all* people, *everywhere*, who accept God and try to live by his law of love. It is a Kingdom within people's hearts. It will come in its fullness at the

end of the world. We can help God's Kingdom to grow by trying to spread love and happiness and by praying for its growth. Discuss.

ACT OF FAITH

Sung, if desired: *CCH* 122 'Holy, holy'.

Or say: Holy, holy, holy Lord, God of power and might. Heaven and earth are full of your glory. Hosannah in the highest.

BIDDING PRAYERS (Response: Thy Kingdom come)
1. Our Father, may your Kingdom grow in our hearts.
2. Our Father, may your Kingdom grow in the hearts of all people.
3. Our Father, may we help to spread happiness in the world.

AT HOME

Each evening with your family, or on your own, reflect on and pray these words: Our Father, who art in heaven, hallowed be thy Name. Thy Kingdom come. Thy will be done on earth as it is in heaven.

Our Father: Session three

POINTS FOR CATECHIST

Read the general notes on the prayer.

Point 3 has separate suggestions for the different age groups. We must careful not to overburden children with world problems, but we should help them to have some sense of responsibility towards the members of God's family who are less fortunate than themselves.

PRESENTATION

1. Refer briefly to the two previous sessions.
2. Say the *Our Father* slowly and prayerfully.
3. *Give us this day our daily bread.* Ask the children what this petition means.

   Why does Jesus use bread here? (It is a basic need.)

   There is an important lesson for us in this petition. Jesus tells us that we should pray for *today's* needs, trusting tomorrow and its needs to God, our Father.

   Is this how we pray?

9–10 years: Does God provide for everybody?
Why does he let people starve?

It is not God, it is people who are responsible for starvation in the world. God provides enough for everyone but people misuse and mismanage God's gifts. They are often greedy and unwilling to share. We, in the Western world, with a relatively small population, use about two-thirds of the world's resources.

We have to ask ourselves:
(a) what do *I* mean when I pray these words?
(b) Do I only think of my own needs, or am I aware of the needs of others?
(c) Am I ever willing to do without— sweets, ice cream, crisps, toys, etc—in order that I may be able to give something to the poor?

If God's family really lived by this petition, would the world be a different and better place?

7–8 years: Do we worry about things unnecessarily?

Will I get a new bike for Christmas?
Will—be my best friend?
Will Dad be cross with me?
Will I get my spellings right?
Will Mum buy me that new dress?

Does worrying ever help? Are we always wanting more, more, more?

Do we pester our parents for money to buy sweets, ice cream, a model aeroplane, a new piece of clothing?

Are we ever willing to do without in order to put some money aside for the poor and hungry?

In what does happiness consist? Do 'things' bring us true happiness?

4. *Forgive us our trespasses as we forgive those who trespass against us.*

Refer to the parable of the unforgiving servant (Matthew 18: 21–25).

The children should remember this parable.

How do we feel about this servant?

Are we sometimes like him, asking God for forgiveness while we bear grudges?

Do we thank God for the way he goes on and on forgiving us?

5. *Lead us not into temptation, but deliver us from evil.*

What is temptation? We are tempted when the idea comes to us to do something wrong. Ask for examples.

Shall I buy sweets with the shopping change without telling Mum? Shall I creep out now it is dark and play outside without anyone knowing?

Temptation only becomes sin if we give in to it. God knows that we are weak and he is ready to help us if we ask him.

Jesus was tempted to do wrong but he never sinned.

ACT OF FAITH AND BIDDING PRAYERS

Pray the *Our Father* together slowly and prayerfully. Different children could pray a petition each.

Or the prayer could be sung.

AT HOME

Each evening this week, with your family or on your own, pray one of these phrases and reflect on it.

Use the prayer: 'Give us this day our daily bread' as a grace before meals this week.

Notes for Lent

NEEDED

Cockfosters Stations of the Cross published by McCrimmons, Vita et Pax 1979.

On card: We adore you, O Christ
and we praise you
because by your holy cross
you have saved the world.

AIM

To make Lent a real preparation for Easter; a time of real growth in our love for Jesus.

1. The importance and meaning of Lent will come through to children in the degree in which this season has meaning for us—

what am *I* doing during Lent to show my love for Christ?

2. Please read through the whole scheme. Each session should be linked with the one before, and each week the children should be reminded of their 'Way of the Cross' at home.

3. The word 'Lent' comes from an old English word meaning 'lengthening of days'.

It is associated with spring, a time of new life and growth, and it should be a happy, not a doleful time.

Ashes have always been a sign of repentance. Ashes are also mixed with earth to help plants grow.

4. In the early Church Lent was a time when people who wanted to become Christians were instructed in the faith. They learnt what it meant to be a follower of Jesus. During Lent, in preparing for Easter, we think about what it means to live like Jesus. It was difficult for the early Christians living in pagan surroundings; it is difficult for us living in a post-christian society. But Jesus has promised to be with us to guide and strengthen us.

5. To help the children keep their thoughts on Jesus, the Lenten scheme follows the Way of the Cross. The material covers two Stations each Sunday. If one Station holds the children's attention, just spend a short while on the second. Our aim is to make each session a prayerful reflection.

On the fifth Sunday in Lent there will be a celebration of the Way of the Cross.

On the sixth Sunday there will be slides showing the last week in Jesus' life.

6. *History of the Stations of the Cross*
   During Holy Week in Jerusalem, the early Christians used to follow the route taken by Jesus from Pilate's residence to Calvary. Along the way they paused for prayer, recalling what had happened to Jesus. The places where they paused were called 'Stations'; these gradually became fixed at fourteen. Over the centuries the custom grew of having pictures of these fourteen Stations inside churches so that Christians, wherever they lived, could follow the Way of the Cross. Some churches have fourteen plain crosses instead of pictures.

7. To help the children pray the Way of the Cross at home, prepare line drawings of the eight Stations:

Pilate condemns Jesus to death
Jesus accepts his cross
Jesus falls beneath the cross
Simon helps Jesus
Jesus meets his mother
The women comfort Jesus
Jesus is stripped of his robe
Jesus dies on the cross.

These can be given out altogether on the Sunday before Lent or two at a time on the appropriate Sundays.

8. *NB* In dealing with the Passion stories we should not stress the *Jews* as being the enemies of Jesus. Speak of the 'leaders' of the people, or of Jesus' enemies. Do not present these stories in a harrowing manner but help the children to enter into the feelings of the people involved.

Sunday before Lent

POINTS FOR CATECHIST

Read the general notes for Lent.

Next Wednesday is Ash Wednesday—Our aim this session is to:—

(a) help the children understand the meaning of Lent;
(b) introduce them to the history and practice of the Stations of the Cross;
(c) encourage them to make their own Way of the Cross each evening at home.

PRESENTATION

1. Reading: Jesus said to them all: 'If anyone wants to come with me, he must forget self, take up his cross everyday, and follow me.' (Luke 9:23, *Good News* version.)

2. Ask the children why the next six weeks are special.

   Does anyone know the origin of the word 'Lent'?

   What is next Wednesday called? Why?

   Why does the Church keep this season?

   Why has this reading been chosen for today?

3. To help us prepare for Jesus' death and Resurrection, we are going to follow the Way of the Cross during Lent.

   Has anyone noticed the Stations in church? How many are there?

   Has anyone made the Stations?

   Does anyone know how this devotion started?

   Why do we make the Stations?

   The general notes for Lent give the history and practice of the Stations of the Cross. Explain how there will be two Stations each week, with a celebration on the fifth Sunday in Lent.

4. Give out the Way of the Cross pictures and explain what the children are to do.

   Each week, at home, colour in the two Stations reflected on during the Sunday session.

   Put the pictures up in your own room or in a public place at home.

   Each evening on your own, or with your family, pray before these Stations.

   There will be

   two Stations for the 1st week in Lent;
   four Stations for the 2nd week in Lent.
   six Stations for the 3rd week in Lent.
   eight Stations for the 4th week in Lent.

   In praying these Stations daily, we will be giving our time to Jesus. We will be doing what He asks of us in today's reading.

ACT OF FAITH

Hymn: 'When I needed a neighbour'. *CCH* 353, v1.

Prayer: Lord Jesus, during Lent may we grow to know you more clearly, love you more dearly and follow you more nearly, day by day.

First Sunday in Lent

The Way of the Cross Pilate condemns Jesus to death. Jesus accepts his cross.

POINTS FOR CATECHIST

Read the general notes for Lent.

The first Station raises the question of why Jesus, who had spent his whole life doing good, should be condemned by his own people. It is clear that he was rejected because he did not conform to their ideas and standards. His ideas on God and religion differed radically from theirs. His was a gospel of love, peace and forgiveness. They were looking for someone who would lead them against the oppressor. Today many followers of Jesus are suffering in prison because they live by his values and do not conform to the world's standards.

Make sure the two Stations and the prayers are pinned up before the start of the session.

PRESENTATION

1. Draw attention to the Stations and remind the children that we will be following the Way of the Cross during Lent.

   Read the passage from the Good News New Testament. Matthew 27: 20–24 (*Good News* version).

   The chief priests and the elders persuaded the crowd to ask Pilate to set Barabbas free and have Jesus put to death. But Pilate asked the crowd: 'Which one of these two do you want me to set free for you?' 'Barabbas,' they answered. 'What, then, shall I do with Jesus called the Messiah?' Pilate asked them.

   'Crucify him!' they all answered. But Pilate asked: 'What crime has he committed?'

   Then they started shouting at the top of their voices: 'Crucify him!' When Pilate saw that it was no use to go on, but that a riot might break out, he took some water, washed his hands in front of the crowd, and said: 'I am not responsible for the death of this man. This is your doing.'

2. *First Station* Pilate condemns Jesus to death.

   Allow a minute for reflection, then ask for comments. If none are forthcoming, prompt the children:

   Who is the man sitting down?
   Who is standing before him? Why?
   Why is Pilate washing his hands?
   Why did he condemn Jesus, if he believed him innocent?
   What has Jesus got on his head? Why?
   What difference do you see between the fists in the picture, and Jesus' hands?
   How does Jesus look? Angry? Sad? Tired? Patient? Afraid?

   9–10 years only
   Why did the leaders reject Jesus?
   Why did they bring him to Pilate?

3. *Second Station* Jesus accepts his cross. Ask for comments.

   Explain that crucifixion was the normal method of execution for a criminal.

   Ask the children to look at Jesus' expression.

   He had spent his life for others, how do you think he is feeling now?

   How do you feel when people turn against you?

   Does Jesus look as if he is accepting his cross?

4. ACT OF FAITH
   Pause for silent reflection and prayer.

   Pray together: 'We adore you, O Christ, and bless you ...'

   Hymn: 'Jesus, we adore you, lay our lives before you. How we love you.' (*SOS* 61)

   Sign of the Cross, slowly and reverently.

5. Remind the children of their Way of the Cross at home. Give out pictures to those who were absent last week.

Second Sunday in Lent

The Way of the Cross. Jesus falls beneath the Cross. Simon helps Jesus.

POINTS FOR THE CATECHIST

Read the general notes for Lent. (Barclay's Commentary on Luke 23: 26 or Mark 15: 21–28.)

In these two Stations we see Jesus identifying himself with the weak, the handicapped, the lonely, the afraid.

Make sure the four Stations and the prayer are pinned up before the session starts.

PRESENTATION

1. Draw attention to the Stations and read the following passage from the *Good News* New Testament, Luke 23: 26.

   'The soldiers led Jesus away, and as they were going, they met a man from Cyrene named Simon who was coming into the city from the country. They seized him, put the cross on him, and made him carry it behind Jesus.'

2. *Third Station*. Jesus falls beneath the cross.

   Allow a minute for reflection, then ask for comments.

   If none are forthcoming prompt the children:
   Why do you think Jesus fell beneath the cross?
   Was he a weak person?
   What kinds of crosses do we have to bear?

   Points for discussion:
   (a) The size and weight of the cross. The Catholic papers usually have photos of pilgrims carrying life-size crosses.

   (b) Jesus' exhaustion after the night trial, scourging and crowning with thorns.
   (c) Jesus' loneliness—the presence of friends strengthens us.
   (d) Our crosses: sickness, pain, loneliness, unpopularity, being misunderstood, etc. How do we cope with them?

3. *Fourth Station*. Simon helps Jesus.

   Ask for comments before questioning the children:

   Who is carrying the cross now? Why?
   Who was Simon?
   How would you feel being ordered to carry a criminal's cross?
   Was it easy for Simon?
   In what ways can we help others to carry their crosses?
   Mum when she has a headache—a friend who is sick—a lonely or unpopular child—the starving, etc.
   How do you feel when asked to help Mum—a friend—someone you don't like?
   Do you ask Jesus to help you carry your cross?

4. ACT OF FAITH
   Pause for silent reflection and prayer.

   Prayer together: 'We adore you, O Christ, and bless you ...'

   Hymn: 'Jesus, we adore you, lay our lives before you. How we love you.' (*SOS* 61)

   Sign of the Cross, slowly and reverently.

5. Remind the children of their Way of the Cross each evening at home.

Third Sunday in Lent

The Way of the Cross. Jesus meets his mother. The women comfort Jesus.

POINTS FOR THE CATECHIST

Read the general notes for Lent.

There is no mention in scripture of Jesus meeting his mother on the way to Calvary but it is part of early Christian tradition. The women who followed Jesus are not named but they must have been people like the widow of Naim, Peter's mother-in-law, the wife of Jairus, and others whom Jesus had helped. Emphasis should be on their desire to show Jesus their love and to bring him comfort and support.

Make sure the six Stations and the prayer are pinned up before the session starts.

PRESENTATION

1. Draw attention to the Stations and read the following: 'Many women followed Jesus weeping, because they felt sorry for him.'

2. *Fifth Station.* Jesus meets his mother.

   Allow a minute for reflection, then ask for comments. If none are forthcoming prompt the children:

   Who is the woman with Jesus?
   Was it easy for Mary to reach Jesus?
   What do we learn about her from this action?
   How do you think Mary was feeling? Sad because unable to do anything for him, glad to be with him to give comfort and support?
   How do you think Jesus felt when his mother reached him? Concerned for her safety—sad that she should see him like this, grateful to her for her courage— strengthened by her presence?
   What do you think they are saying to each other?
   Do you like to have Mummy with you when you are ill, lonely or unhappy?

3. *Sixth Station.* The women comfort Jesus. Ask for comments before asking:

   Who were these women? Why had they struggled through the crowd?
   Did they help Jesus? How?
   Look at Jesus. Is he thinking about himself or others?
   Do we notice when other people need help?
   Are we brave enough to help a friend in need?

4. ACT OF FAITH

   Pause for silent reflection and prayer.
   Pray together: 'We adore you, O Christ and bless you ...'

   Hymn: 'Jesus, we adore you, lay our lives before you. How we love you.' (*SOS* 61)

   Sign of the Cross, slowly and reverently.

5. Remind the children of their Way of the Cross each evening at home.

Fourth Sunday in Lent

The Way of the Cross. Jesus is stripped of his robe. Jesus dies on the cross.

POINTS FOR THE CATECHIST

Read the general notes for Lent. (Barclay's Commentary on Mark 15: 29–4, or Luke 23: 32–38.) Points for Catechist, 1st Sunday in Lent, dealing with the question of why Jesus was rejected by the people.

The main emphasis this week is on the last Station in which Jesus fulfils his own words: 'The greatest love a person can have for his friends is to give his life for them.'

INRI: in Latin these initials stand for Jesus of Nazareth, King of the Jews.

PRESENTATION

1. Draw attention to the Stations and then read the following passage taken from Luke and John (adapted from several versions):

   When they came to the place of the Skull they crucified Jesus.

   Pilate had a notice fastened to the Cross. It, read: 'Jesus of Nazareth, King of the Jews.

   When they had crucified Jesus the soldiers shared out his clothing amongst themselves.

   All this time his mother was standing near the cross with John, his dearly loved friend. Jesus said to his mother: 'Mother, take my friend as your son.' Then he said to his friend: 'Take my mother as your own mother.'

   And from that time John took Mary home and looked after her.

   Before he died, Jesus also prayed for his enemies who were crucifying him. This was his prayer: 'Father, forgive them. They do not know what they are doing.'

2. *Seventh Station* Jesus is stripped of his robe.

Allow a minute for reflection and then ask for comments.

There is deep symbolism in this Station. In being stripped of his robe, Jesus is being stripped of all his material possessions. His greatest possession, his *love*, could never be taken from him. The next Station shows him still loving his Father, still loving and forgiving people.

3. *Eighth Station*. Jesus dies on the cross.

   Ask for comments. If none are forthcoming, prompt the children:

   Who are the two people with Jesus?
   What does their presence at the foot of the cross tell us about them?
   What is Jesus saying to them?
   Is Jesus thinking about Himself in His suffering?
   Is it easy to think of others when we are in pain or unhappy?
   What do we learn about Jesus from his prayer on the cross?
   Do we find it easy to forgive people who hurt us?
   Do we ask Jesus to help us to forgive?
   Have you ever noticed the letters INRI on a crucifix?
   What do they stand for?
   When you see Jesus' arm stretched out on the cross, what does this say to you?

4. ACT OF FAITH

   Pause for silent reflection and prayer.

   Pray together: 'We adore you, O Christ and bless you ...'

   Hymn: 'Jesus, we adore you, lay our lives before you. How we love you.' (*SOS* 61)

5. Remind the children of their Way of the Cross each evening at home.

Fifth Sunday in Lent

The Way of the Cross

Needed: Eight Stations of the Cross. Picture of the Resurrection. Prayer: 'We adore you, O Christ, and we praise you, because by your holy cross you have saved the world.' Large candle. Papers for children who are reading.

POINTS FOR CATECHIST

Pin up the eight Stations and the prayer but *not* the picture of the Resurrection. Explain that we are going to follow the Way of the Cross, pausing like the early Christians to ... look at the Station—think of the event—
Tell Jesus of our love—pray together.

Give papers to the children who are going to read. Explain to the group exactly what is going to happen and make sure the readers know what to do. The celebration should be reverent and prayerful.

CELEBRATION

Light the Christ candle.
Sign of the Cross together.

1st child	First Station.
2nd child	Pilate condemns Jesus.
All	We adore you, O Christ...
Leader	Ask a child to comment on the Station.
Pause	for silent prayer.
Leader	For the times we have blamed other people, especially when it was not their fault
All	We are sorry, Lord Jesus.
Sing	Jesus, we adore you, lay our lives before you. How we love you.
3rd child	Second Station.
4th child	Jesus accepts his cross.
All	We adore you, O Christ...
Leader	Ask a child to comment on the Station.
Pause	for silent prayer.
Leader	For the times we have grumbled about our difficulties and troubles
All	We are sorry, Lord Jesus
Sing	Jesus, we adore you...

5th child	Third Station.
6th child	Jesus falls beneath his cross.
All	We adore you, O Christ...
Leader	Ask a child to comment on the Station.
Pause	for silent prayer.
Leader	For the times we have teased others and made them unhappy
All	We are sorry, Lord Jesus.
Sing	Jesus, we adore you...
7th child	Fourth Station.
8th child	Simon helps Jesus.
All	We adore you, O Christ...
Leader	Ask a child to comment on the Station.
Pause	for silent prayer.
Leader	For the times we have refused to help others
All	We are sorry, Lord Jesus.
Sing	Jesus, we adore you...
9th child	Fifth Station.
10th child	Jesus meets his Mother.
All	We adore you, O Christ...
Leader	Ask a child to comment on the Station.
Pause	for silent prayer.
Leader	For the times when we've acted as if we did not love Mummy.
All	We are sorry, Lord Jesus.
Sing	Jesus, we adore you...
11th child	Sixth Station.
12th child	The women comfort Jesus.
All	We adore you, O Christ...
Leader	Ask a child to comment on the Station.
Pause	for silent prayer.
Leader	For the times we have not bothered to comfort someone who was feeling sad.
All	We are sorry, Lord Jesus.
Sing	Jesus, we adore you...
13th child	Seventh Station.
14th child	Jesus is stripped of his robe.
All	We adore you, O Christ...

Leader	Ask a child to comment on the Station.
Pause	for silent prayer.
Leader	For the times we have taken something which did not belong to us.
All	We are sorry, Lord Jesus.
Sing	Jesus, we adore you...

15th child	Eighth Station.
16th child	Jesus dies on the cross.

Blow out the candle.

All	We adore you, O Christ...
Leader	Ask a child to comment on the Station.
Pause	For silent prayer.
Leader	For all the times when we have done wrong.
All	We are sorry, Lord Jesus.
Sing	Jesus, we adore you...

Leader	Dear Jesus, we thank you for your great love; We thank you for your forgiveness. We want to show you our love during the next two weeks of Lent. Please help us to follow our Way of the Cross at home. Amen.
Pause	for a moment's silent thanksgiving.
Hymn	'Were you there when they crucified my lord?' (*CCH*347.)
Leader	We know Jesus' death was not the end, and so before we go we pin up the picture of the Resurrection and re-light the Christ Candle. This reminds us that Jesus was victorious over sin and death.

End with a reverent and prayerful sign of the cross together.

Notes for Eastertide

The Easter message is not that Jesus *rose* but that Jesus *is risen* and is *with us now*.

We should ask ourselves: Do I think of the Resurrection in this way? Is Jesus a *living* presence in my life? If Jesus had not risen, would it make any difference to me?

The spirit of Easter is a spirit of *joy* and *peace* because Jesus' message is always 'Peace be with you, I'm here, don't be frightened.'

The celebration for Easter Sunday speaks for itself without much explanation. The large candle represents Jesus, the Light of the World, who has conquered darkness and sin. The Easter garden is to remind us of the new life all around us, and the Easter eggs are a sign of the new life which they contain within themselves.

Alleluia is an Easter word.

All the Easter stories lend themselves to dramatisation.

SCHEME

Easter Sunday	Celebration
Easter 2	No groups—holidays
Easter 3	Jesus comes to his friends
Easter 4	Jesus and Thomas
Easter 5	The Good Shepherd
Easter 6	The lakeside meal
Easter 7	The secret of happiness
Optional	Celebration of life and growth. One Sunday is needed in preparation.

Easter celebration

PREPARATION

Pin up:

The words of the prayer 'Jesus is Alive';

The words of the hymns 'Sing Alleluia to the Lord' (*CCH* 712, v2); 'This is the Day' (*CCH* 625, v1); 'Alleluia, Alleluia, give thanks' (*CCH* 395, chorus).

Pin up and *veil* a large picture of the Resurrection; a card with the threefold Alleluia printed on it.

Place on the altar a large Christ candle, some nightlights, some painted eggs or Easter eggs, and an Easter garden. Cover the latter.

Leader: Explain that this is an Easter celebration full of Alleluias because Alleluia is an Easter word meaning Hooray! We try and enter into the feelings of the women on Easter morning and make our singing and responses joyful. Tell the children to notice (1) when the candle is lit; (2) when the covers are removed.

CELEBRATION

Hymn: 'This is the Day', verse 1 (unveil Alleluia).

Reading: *Listen*, No 39 P82, adapted.

Reader A: On Sunday morning, very early (light candle, and nightlights)—just as the sun was beginning to shine—Mary Magdalen, Salome, and Mary, the mother of James, went to the cave where Jesus was buried. They had been saying to one another:

Reader B: 'Who will roll away the stone for us from the entrance to the tomb?'

Reader A: But when they got there, they found the great boulder had been rolled away from the door, and when they went inside, they found a young man there, dressed all in white. At first they were afraid when they saw him, so he said:

Reader C: 'Don't be frightened (unveil resurrection picture); You want Jesus who was killed, don't you? Well, you can see where they put him, but he's not here now. He is alive. Go and tell Peter and the others they will see him in Galilee.'

Reader A: Then the women came out of the cave (uncover garden and eggs) and, filled with great wonder and joy, they ran to tell the disciples.

Leader: This is the Gospel of the Lord.

All: Praise to you, Lord Jesus Christ!

Hymn: 'This is the day, this is the day, that he rose again.'

Leader Ask the children if they noticed when the candle was lit, the Alleluias and picture were uncovered, the garden and eggs were uncovered. Do they know why we have Easter eggs—an Easter garden? Do they remember the angel's message? How did the women feel? What did they do? Do we feel joyful today? Why?

PROCESSION

Leader: Explain that we are going to walk round the altar, clapping our hands for joy and singing the Easter message to each other: 'Sing Alleluia to the Lord' and 'Jesus is risen from the dead.' When back in our places, we will give each other the sign of Easter Peace.

Prayer: The lines are read by different children.
The group respond with 'Alleluia!'

Jesus is alive. Alleluia!
He is with us now. Alleluia!
He says, 'Peace be with you.' Alleluia!

'There is nothing to fear.' Alleluia!
Everything is all right. Alleluia!
God loves us always. Alleluia!
Praise him, praise him. Alleluia!

Sing: 'Alleluia, alleluia, give thanks to the Risen Lord'—chorus.

Leader: We end with the special sign we have as followers of Jesus—the sign of the cross.

SOMETHING TO DO AT HOME

Either make an Easter garden, *or* make an Easter candle for the table. Get a thick white candle about 18 inches high. Decorate it with a cross, the year, and an Alleluia.

Easter 3: Jesus comes to his friends

READING: *Listen* No 41 (P86), Doubting Thomas. John 20: 19–23.

On the evening of the same day, Jesus came and showed himself to them all. It happened like this.

Some of the followers of Jesus were sitting together talking. They had locked the doors behind them because they were afraid they might be arrested like Jesus. But Jesus just came straight in and said: 'Hello.'

'Peace be with you,' he said, and he showed them the wounds in his hands and his side. It was *great* to see him again.

Then Jesus said: 'My Father has sent me to you. Now I am sending you to help others. I give you the Holy Spirit to help you to do this.' And he breathed on them.

'In future,' he said, 'If you forgive people, I will forgive them as well.'

POINTS FOR CATECHIST

Barclay: John 20: 19–23.

It is important to set the scene for the children. The apostles must have been feeling wretched. Their Master had died a terrible death, forsaken by them in his hour of need. They were sad at losing him, and unable to forgive themselves for their cowardice; their hopes were shattered.

The Risen Jesus comes into this scene with his message of peace. Rejected by his enemies and forsaken by his friends, he brings his message of reconciliation. We all have the experience of someone having brought peace to us when we have felt utterly forsaken; children will also have some experience of this. Jesus crowns his reconciliation by giving them the gift of his Spirit and the power to continue his work of forgiving sin. The apostles' surprise and joy must have been overwhelming.

Notice that St John has Jesus giving the Spirit on Easter Sunday, not at Pentecost as in the Acts of the Apostles.

Dramatising this scene will help children enter into the joy of the Resurrection.

PRESENTATION

1. Set the scene for the reading by getting the children to imagine they are the apostles in the upper room. They have all run away when their Master was arrested and they are wondering whether the authorities are searching for them. How do they feel? They were too cowardly to stand by him in his great need. How do they feel? Pause for silent reflection.

   Gospel Reading.

2. Let the children express how they feel; then act out the scene. Draw attention to:
   (a) Jesus' message of peace—how differently we react when everyone is against us, or when a friend lets us down!
   (b) Jesus shows them his hands and his side. This is important in view of next week's session.
   (c) Jesus gives them the power to carry on his work of forgiving sin; of reconciling people with God and with each other.
   (d) Thomas was absent. How would they feel about this?

3. *If time*, 9–10 yrs:
   Refer to the Sacrament of Reconciliation. When do priests exercise this power of forgiving sin? How do we feel when we have received this Sacrament? Jesus said: 'Peace be with you.' In this Sacrament the priest says: 'Go in peace.' What does he mean?

ACT OF FAITH

CCH 257, verse 1, 'Peace, perfect peace.' While singing, the Sign of Peace is given to one another.

BIDDING PRAYERS

We remember how Jesus forgave his friends and we pray: 'Our Father, who art in heaven, forgive us our trespasses, as we forgive those who trespass against us. Amen.'

Easter 4: Jesus and Thomas

READING: *Listen* No 41B (P87). John 20: 24–29.

Thomas the Twin wasn't there when Jesus came the first time, and when he came back they told him: 'We have seen Jesus.' But he said: 'I will not believe it, until I have seen him for myself.'

One week later, Jesus came to them all a second time, and he said to Thomas: 'Look! Here are my hands. Hold them! Feel the wound on my side, as well!' And Thomas said: 'You are my Lord and my God!'

Then Jesus said: 'You know that I am alive because you can see me. May God bless all those people who will not be able to see me but will still believe in me!'

POINTS FOR CATECHIST

Before reading the commentary, reflect on what this passage says to *you* about (1) Jesus; (2) Thomas.

Barclay: John 20: 24–29.

It is *essential* that this session be closely linked with the previous one, as the two readings are part of one Gospel story. Dramatisation will help the children enter into the feelings of the characters involved. Note how Jesus understood Thomas with all his failings. He came again especially for Thomas and led him from doubt to faith.

PRESENTATION

1. Tell the children to imagine the scene as it is being read so that they will be ready to act it. Begin with last week's reading if you wish.

   Gospel reading.

2. Discuss briefly the different characters:

The apostles—so thrilled, longing to share their joy with Thomas; a little smug perhaps?

Thomas—solitary and obstinate in his misery—rejoining the group for support. Angry perhaps with himself for what he had missed, with Jesus for coming when he wasn't there. Jealous of his friends? He still loved Jesus; he longed to believe.

Jesus—understanding and accepting Thomas, coming specially for him.

3. Reflect with the children on how you would feel in Thomas' situation.

   How do we feel if we miss a special occasion through our own fault?
   How do we behave when upset?
   How do we feel when Jesus comes to us in Holy Communion?

   Be ready to accept very different reactions and feelings from the children.

4. Dramatise the story. This can be done straight after the Gospel reading, before any discussion, if preferred.

5. *If time*, discuss: Is it easier for us to believe in Jesus today, than it was for the apostles and those who lived at that time?

ACT OF FAITH

SOS 61, *Hymn*: 'Jesus, we adore you, lay our lives before you. How we love you.'

BIDDING PRAYERS (Lord Jesus, please be with them.)

1. We pray for all those who are lonely and miserable.

2. We pray for all those who are suffering from the death of someone they love, especially anyone we know. . . .

3. We pray for all those who find it hard to believe in God.

SOMETHING TO DO

At the Consecration, when the bell rings, and the priest raises the Host and the chalice, pray silently: 'My Lord and my God.'
Use the same prayer after Communion.

Easter 5: The Good Shepherd

READING: *Listen* No 7B (P23), The shepherd and his sheep. John 10: 1–15.

One day Jesus said: 'Sheep listen to their own shepherd and they will follow him. He can even call them one by one, for he knows their names, and he can call them out of the sheepfold through the gate.

'When they have all come out, he walks in front of them, and they all follow because they know the sound of his voice.

'Of course, they would never follow a stranger because they would not know the sound of his voice. They would run away from him if he told them to follow him.'

Then Jesus said: 'I am a shepherd and I'm the *Good* Shepherd. I know all my sheep, every one of them, and they know me.

POINTS FOR CATECHIST

Barclay: John 10: 1–15 has useful material on Palestinian shepherds. *Getting to Know About Farming and Fishing* has excellent illustrations.

The Israelites were originally a nomadic people herding flocks of sheep and goats. It was natural for them to think of God as a shepherd. In Ezekiel Ch 34 the prophet has a beautiful description of God as the shepherd of his people: 'I myself will pasture my sheep, I myself will show them where to rest—it is the Lord Yahweh who speaks. I shall look for the lost one, bring back the stray, bandage the wounded and make the weak strong. I shall watch over the fat and healthy. I shall be a true Shepherd to them.' (*Jerusalem Bible*)

Jesus would have had this passage in mind, as well as Psalm 23, when he spoke of himself as the Good Shepherd.

PRESENTATION

1. Gospel reading.

2. Discuss the work of a shepherd in Europe and compare it with that of a shepherd in Palestine. The life of a Palestinian shepherd today would be very similar to what it was in the time of Jesus. Draw on any experience the children may have of shepherds, either at first hand or from TV. They may have watched sheepdog trials. A shepherd feeds, guides, cares for, guards and marks or brands his sheep. Is it a responsible job? What would happen if the shepherd were careless?

3. Jesus calls himself the Good Shepherd. What does he mean by this? Who are his sheep? Quote from Ezekiel if you wish.

4. Shepherds lead, sheep follow. What other groups of leaders and followers can you think of? Parents—children. Teachers—pupils. Drivers—passengers. Doctors—patients. Etc.

   Jesus died to save his sheep. Would a parent, teacher, driver die to protect his charges? Who is the chief shepherd of Jesus' flock today?

5. *7–8 years* could act out this parable, children taking the parts of the shepherd, his dog, wolves, robbers, sheep and the one stray sheep. The sheep can be led to pasture, counted, brought home to the fold, have their wounds washed, etc.

ACT OF FAITH

Praise! No 34 (Response: Lord, I am safe with you.)

Lord, you look after me, I am safe with you. (Response)

I go to bed at night and fall asleep and nothing worries me. (Response)

I wake up safe and sound, for *you* protect me. (Response)

BIDDING PRAYERS (Lord Jesus, be their shepherd and guide.)

1. We pray for the leaders of nations.

2. We pray for our Holy Father the Pope, and for our *Bishop*.

3. We pray for all priests, especially for Father— and Father—.

SOMETHING TO DO, 7–8 years

Draw and cut out a sheep. Write your name on it. Pin it on your lapel or hang it in your room as a sign that you are one of Jesus' sheep.

Easter 6: The lakeside meal

READING: *New World* Pp409–410. John 21: 1–18.

After this Jesus showed himself again to his friends. This is what happened on the beach of Galilee Lake. Seven of his friends were together there—Peter, Thomas 'the twin', Nathanael from Cana, Zebedee's sons (James and John) and two other of his friends.

'I'm taking the boat out fishing,' said Peter. 'We'll come along with you,' said the others. They all got into the boat there and then.

They were out all night and now the day was breaking. Jesus stood on the beach. Nobody recognised him. 'Lads,' he called out, 'have you had any luck?' 'Not a fish,' they called back. 'Try the starboard side,' he called. 'There's fish there.'

Out went the net. The mass of fish they got was so great they could not haul the net in.

'It's Jesus,' said the friend whom Jesus loved dearly, to Peter. Peter had been fishing naked. When he heard the name Jesus he flung his cloak round him and jumped into the water. The others brought the boat in, dragging the net. They were only about a hundred yards off shore.

They got out of the boat—and there was a charcoal fire burning on the beach, and fish cooking on it; there was bread, too. 'Get some of the fish you've just caught,' said Jesus.

Peter went on board and dragged the net to the shore. The net had not been torn, in spite of the mass of fish.

'Let's have breakfast,' said Jesus. Nobody dared ask him who he was.

Jesus picked up the bread and the fish and gave them to his friends. After breakfast Jesus turned to Peter as they walked along, and called him by his own name Simon. 'Simon,' he said, 'do you love me more than anything else?' 'Yes, sir,' said Peter, 'you know I love you.' 'Look after my friends,' said Jesus.

Jesus spoke to Peter a second time. 'Simon,' he said, 'do you love me?' 'Yes, sir,' said Peter, 'you know I love you.' 'Look after my friends,' said Jesus.

Then a third time Jesus spoke to Peter, 'Simon,' he said, 'do you love me?' For Jesus to ask him this question three times upset Peter. 'Sir,' he said, 'you know all about me. You, of all people, know I love you.'

'Look after my friends,' said Jesus.

POINTS FOR CATECHIST

Barclay: John 21: 1–18

Getting to Know About Farming and Fishing has useful material on Galilean fishermen.

This story is about the mystery of the Risen Jesus; the unexpected transformation of failure into success. There is the contrast between the unlikely material and the superabundant outcome. God can work through our weakness if we trust him.

The Risen Jesus is the same Lord who washed his disciples' feet. Here he is seen serving his friends with a meal. If Peter is to lead the flock he must follow his Master's way of service.

Jesus' authority is felt in this story. These men were professional fishermen who knew the lake and the habits of the fish; yet at the word of a 'stranger' they let down their nets once more.

This is an excellent story for dramatisation.

PRESENTATION

1. Gospel reading.

2. Discuss the scene:

(a) The apostles shaken by events feel aimless. Peter, still their leader, makes a decision: 'Let's get back to work.' How would we feel after a night's fishing with no results?

(b) Jesus comes to reassure, to help, to guide. How would we have reacted when told to lower our nets again? Because they trusted and obeyed, he was able to help them.

(c) They don't recognise Jesus. Were they too upset, too preoccupied? What does Peter *do* when he recognises Jesus?

(d) Why does Jesus ask Peter *three* times if he loved him?

3. How is Jesus with us in our daily life?

Do we recognise him?

When does he give us the opportunity of expressing our sorrow for the times when we have let him down?

4. Dramatise the story.

ACT OF FAITH

Hymn: 'Haul, haul away' (*CCH* 114); *or Prayer*: Dear Jesus, may we know you more clearly, love you more dearly, and follow you more nearly, day by day.

BIDDING PRAYERS (Lord Jesus, watch over them.)

1. We pray for all sailors and their families.

2. We pray for all lifeboat-men who risk their lives for others.

3. We pray for all fishermen who work so hard to catch fish for us.

Easter 7: The secret of happiness

READING: *New World* P397. John 15: 11–17.

'In talking to you as I have done,' said Jesus, 'I have had one aim in view: I wanted you to know the happiness I know. I don't want anything to spoil your happiness. This is the secret of it—my secret, your secret: love one another as I have loved you. For a man to die for his friends—that is the greatest love we know. You

are real friends of mine—if you do what I have told you.

'I don't want you to be my "slaves", just doing the things you are told to do, without knowing at all why you are doing them. I want you to be my "friends": that's why I shared with you all I have learned from my Father.

'You did not choose me, you remember; I chose you. And I chose you for one purpose: I want you to go on growing, producing a rich and lasting harvest.

'This then is my order: love one another in the same way as I have loved you.'

POINTS FOR CATECHIST

Barclay: John 15: 11–17.

The secret of Jesus' happiness was (1) The knowledge of his Father's love for him; and (2) his own response in selfless love. He gave himself totally to God and to people.

He wants us to share in his happiness and to pass it on to others. We need to stop and ask ourselves:

Do we ever put people off by a negative attitude towards God and religion?

Do we see our religion as a set of rules to be obeyed or as a relationship to be lived?

Are we sad or happy in our following of Jesus?

Do we really believe that God loves us?

Do *we* try to keep this commandment of Jesus?

PRESENTATION

1. Gospel reading.

2. Do you like this reading? Why?.

3. 'I want you to know the happiness I know.'

   Discuss the secret of Jesus' happiness.
   (a) What made him a happy person?
   (b) Did being happy mean he never suffered, was never upset, always had time to do what he wanted, always found things easy?
   We know he cried at a friend's death (Lazarus); was weary by a well; was betrayed by a friend, sometimes had hardly time to eat.

4. 'I don't want anything to spoil your happiness.'

   Discuss
   (a) The things that make us truly happy.
   (b) The things that make us unhappy.

(c) Who are the people who bring us joy?
(d) How do we try to make other people happy?

Help the children to reflect on their own experience of the happiness they feel when they act unselfishly.

5. Jesus says to his apostles, and he also says to us:

   'You did not choose me: I chose you.'

   Discuss:
   (a) Why did he choose these men? Was it because they were rich, clever, good? What did he want of them?
   (b) Why did Jesus choose us? What does he want of us?
   (c) What did he order them to do?
   (d) How can we, at our age, carry out Jesus' command of love?

ACT OF FAITH (*Grail Prayer*)
Each line can be said by a child or group of children:

Lord Jesus,
I give you my hands to do your work.
I give you my feet to go your way.
I give you my eyes to see as you do.
I give you my tongue to speak your words.
I give you my mind that you may think in me.
Above all, I give you my heart, that you may love in me your Father, and all mankind.

Or 'Give me love in my heart ...' (*CCH* 84, verse 3)

BIDDING PRAYERS (Lord, help them to show forth your happiness.)

1. We pray for all Christians in our neighbourhood.

2. We pray for those who are preaching your Word to people who don't know about you.

3. We pray for all those who are preparing to be baptised or who have just been baptised.

Life and growth

Listen! (Page 18) No 4. Isaiah 27: 3–6.
God says:

> I am a Gardener
> and I look after my garden
> all day and all night.
>
> I keep watering all my plants
> because I don't want them to dry up
> or their leaves will fall off.
>
> If I find any weeds,
> I will pull them up and burn them.
>   Then the whole of my garden will be
> filled with flowers.

POINTS FOR CATECHIST

This session is a preparation for next week's celebration of life and growth, in which the children will each bring one thing they like doing. We helped them enter into the spirit of Lent, now we help them enter into the joy of Eastertide, the joy of new life and growth. We see new life and growth all around us, and the reading shows how growth has to be nurtured. God gives us powers or gifts. For them to bear fruit, we have to use them.

PRESENTATION

1. Reading

2. Very briefly introduce the idea of life and growth from the new life we see around us: buds, bulbs, blossom, lambs, birds nesting, bees humming, animals and insects waking from hibernation. In winter everything seems dead; but life is there and growth has been going on secretly.

3. Discuss their own growth. Like seeds we are planted in the world. We don't see growth taking place (hair, nails ...). But gradually we are aware of it—things we can do now which we couldn't do before, or couldn't do so well. We all have gifts and we have to 'water' them, care for them if they are to grow and produce fruit.

Discuss their individual gifts; the things they especially like doing. Explain that next Sunday we are going to celebrate our gifts. Each person will choose *one* thing they like doing: painting, cooking, playing an instrument, constructing Lego, writing or reciting poetry, photography, caring for baby, chess or other games, etc.

Pause while each child decides what they will bring; they now say what it will be. Tell them *not to forget* to bring their gift.

NB: They can bring a musical instrument and talk about it if they don't feel able to play it.

ACT OF FAITH

On card (from *Listen!* No 17B, last line adapted):

> I want to tell the whole wide world
>   God has been good to me!
> I want to tell the whole wide world
>   God is wonderful!
> I want to shout and sing because I am so happy!
> Jesus is risen from the dead!

Hymn: 'All that I am' (*CCH* 11, v1); *or* 'Sing it in the valleys' (*AK* 84). (Words on card.)

Celebration of life and growth

Remind the children that we have come together to celebrate—to thank God for the gifts, the powers which he gives to each of us. Gifts which we often take for granted. It's a *celebration* and therefore our singing and responses should be *joyful!*

It would be meaningful if the catechists brought their own gifts as well.

CELEBRATION

All: God is very good to us. Let's praise him! (on card)

Sing: Alleluia, alleluia, give thanks to God our Father,
Alleluia, alleluia, give praise to his Name! (*CCH* 395, adapted; on card)

Reading: Listen! (P18) No 4.

Response: God is very good to us. Let's praise him!

The catechist then introduces each child with:
Let's praise God with ------ (music, painting, helpfulness, crafts) . . . A child shows a gift, saying: 'I'm -----, and I like ------'

(they can play or recite, or say a word about it).

As the gift is put on the altar . . .

All: Thank you God for (Jim's) gift.

When all the children have shown their gifts:

All: I want to tell the whole wide world
God has been good to me!
I want to tell the whole wide world
God is wonderful!
I want to shout and sing because I am so happy!
Jesus is risen from the dead!

Sing: Alleluia, alleluia, give thanks to God our Father,
Alleluia, alleluia, give praise to his Name.

NB: The celebration need not be as formal as this. The children can simply show or play their gifts in turn, and then talk about them afterwards. The hymns 'All that I am' and 'Sing it in the valleys' are both suitable.

Notes for Whitsuntide

The aim of this scheme is to help the children understand the work of the Holy Spirit in the early Church. Jesus promised to send his Spirit of Truth, the Comforter, to his friends. The Spirit would make clear to them all that Jesus had taught them and would give them strength to witness to the truth. These stories show how the disciples changed from being frightened and bewildered to being men of courage; convinced of the truth of their message and happy to suffer for their Master.

To get the feel of these Pentecost experiences it would be helpful to read the whole of the Acts of the Apostles. This book was written by St Luke as a continuation of his Gospel (Good News). Luke presents us with an idealised picture of the early Christian community. St Paul's Epistles (especially his letters to the Corinthians) show rather a different picture of these same communities struggling to reach their ideal, not always successfully.

The clash between the early Christians and the Jewish authorities needs to be carefully dealt with to avoid children getting a wrong idea of the Jews. The clash was inevitable. The Jews believed they were the chosen people but failed to understand their mission—of bringing all men to God. Jesus and his followers preached the universality of God's love. When referring to the opposition of the authorities it is better to speak of the leaders of the people rather than of the Jewish leaders.

NB. This scheme has excellent material for dramatisation or mime.

1. Jesus gives the promised Spirit to his Church. The Great Day.

2. The Spirit at work in the early Christian community. How the Friends of Jesus lived.

3. Peter heals through the power of the Spirit. Clash with the Leaders.

4. The friends of Jesus receive courage through the power of the Spirit. Prison Again.

5. The friends of Jesus pray in the power of the Spirit. Trouble Again.

6. The power of the Spirit at work in Stephen. Stephen's Arrest.

7. Saul is changed by the power of the Spirit. Saul on the Road.

8. Paul receives courage through the power of the Spirit. He meets the Friends of Jesus.

Pentecost

READING: The Great Day (*New World* Pp163–166, adapted). Acts 2: 1–41.

It was now the time of the Feast, 'the Fiftieth Day' (Pentecost), when Jewish people remembered how Moses gave them God's Law on Mount Sinai.

The friends of Jesus were all together in the house where they were staying. Then it happened. Suddenly, as if a storm of wind and fire burst upon them, they were all filled with God's own power and they began to talk in many strange ways. God gave them the power to speak out boldly.

Jewish pilgrims from lands all over the world were staying in Jerusalem City; they came from Mesopotamia in the East, from the shores of the Black Sea in the North, from Egypt in the South and even from Rome in the West.

A great crowd gathered, talking excitedly; they were amazed and didn't know what to think. 'What's all this about?' they were asking.

Peter stood up, and the other close friends of Jesus stood with him. He shouted over the noise of the crowd: 'Fellow countrymen, listen to me. This is something you all ought to know about—so listen to me. You yourselves know all about Jesus of Nazareth. He lived and worked among you. All he did was proof enough that God sent him and that God was with him. You handed him over to the Romans and killed him, but God raised him to life again; death could not be the end of his work. All of us here have met him and been with him since his death and know he is alive. Long ago God promised to give us his own power in our hearts; he has kept his promise and through Jesus he has given us his power. You must change your ways and join the company of the Friends of Jesus. God will give you the power of His Spirit in your hearts.'

And about three thousand people accepted what Peter said, and joined the company of the Friends of Jesus.

POINTS FOR CATECHIST

Barclay: Acts 2: 1–41. *Getting to Know About Festivals*, P11.

Pentecost was a Jewish feast occurring fifty days after the Feast of Passover; so Jerusalem was full of pilgrims.

The importance of this feast for Christians is the transforming power of the Holy Spirit. The terrified disciples are filled with the courage to go out and proclaim their message that Jesus is alive. Notice that they were praying at the time.

Wind: Invisible and unpredictable. It is seen in its effects—smoke, weather vanes, trees, etc. A source of power; used for sailing ships, water wheels, windmills, etc. Moves clouds. As breath: breath of life through mouth-to-mouth resuscitation.

Fire: Cleanses, purifies, sterilises. Unifies and mends by welding; moulds by softening metal and glass; transforms, eg iron into steel; illuminates—warms—comforts.

PRESENTATION:

1. Reading.
2. What were the friends of Jesus doing when the Holy Spirit came?
3. Why did the Holy Spirit come under the signs of wind and fire? What was God trying to show? Draw out the symbolism.
4. 'God gave them power to speak out boldly.' Do you notice any difference in the disciples before and after the coming of the Holy Spirit?
   It is only fifty days since they all ran away when Jesus was arrested in the Garden. During the next few weeks the readings will show how the Holy Spirit helped the friends of Jesus in different ways.

ACT OF FAITH

CCH 457. 'Fear not, rejoice and be glad.' Chorus. Or: 'We believe in the Holy Spirit, the Lord the giver of Life. Alleluia!'

BIDDING PRAYERS (Lord Jesus, please give them your Spirit of Wisdom and Love.)

1. We pray for all bishops, especially for our own bishop.
2. We pray for the leaders of the world.
3. We pray for everyone in our parish.

Pentecost 2

READING: How the friends of Jesus Lived. (*New World* Pp166–167, adapted). Acts 2: 42–47; 4: 32–37; 5: 14–16.

The friends of Jesus made a great stir in the city. They lived day by day in God's Way as Jesus had shown them; Peter and James and John explained it to them.

They lived together like members of one family. When they had supper together, they broke bread, shared it as Jesus had done at the last supper on the night before he died, and remembered what Jesus had done for everybody everywhere.

They spent much time in prayer.

They lived together and shared everything with one another. They sold their property and possessions and shared the money out so that nobody went without anything he needed. Every day they went to Temple worship, and met at home to 'break bread' together. They shared their meals together with real happiness. All this was their way of thanking God for all he had done for them. The people in the city thought well of them. Day by day, with God's help, their numbers grew. They were one in heart and mind, and none of them thought that his own things were just for his own use— they were for everybody to share. So the close friends of Jesus, like Peter, made it very clear what 'Jesus being alive again' really meant.

They were a happy company. Nobody went without what he needed. The rich people among them sold their lands and houses, and brought the money they got to their leaders. It was then shared out as each had need. Here is an example. One of them, Joseph, was a rich man (Peter and his friends called him Barnabas). He was born in the island of Cyprus but he worked in the Temple, helping in the services there. He owned a field. He went and sold it and brought the money to the leaders.

More and more people, crowds of men and women, believed in Jesus and joined his company of friends. Just as Jesus healed those who were ill, so did his friends. People brought sick people on beds and mats out into the streets. 'Peter's shadow will fall on them as he walks along,' they said. They brought the sick from villages outside the city, too.

POINTS FOR CATECHIST

Barclay: Acts 2: 42–47; 4: 32–37; 5: 14–16.

This reading gives the ideal by which these early Christians lived. Theirs was true communism bringing great happiness, but it was no more easy for them to share their belongings than it is for us. The Holy Spirit is as willing to help us as He was to help them. They still worshipped in the Temple and were steeped in the Jewish tradition of worship; our Liturgy of the Word is based on their synagogue service. The Eucharist was celebrated in their homes because there were no churches. House Masses are not an innovation!

PRESENTATION:

1. Read the passage, allowing for comment as you read.

2. 'The friends of Jesus made a great stir in the city!' Discuss. Could this reading be applied to (a) our parish; (b) God's world-wide family?

   If we lived like this would we make a stir in our city? Would the world be a happier place? Why do we find it so difficult to share our possessions? Was it easier for the early Christians than it is for us? Where did their strength come from?

   What do we call people who live together in community sharing their money and possessions? Do you know any monks or nuns?

3. They were a happy company. Why were they happy? Are we happy to be friends of Jesus when things are difficult?

   Do we grumble when: it is time for church or for prayer; we are asked to share our things or our time; it is suggested that we share our money with the poor?

4. They met at home to 'break bread' together. What were they doing and why

did they use this expression? Why was Mass celebrated in their homes rather than in church? Have you ever been to a house Mass? What was it like?

ACT OF FAITH

SOS 69 'Bind us together'; *or AK* 73 'The Beatitudes'.

BIDDING PRAYERS (Lord, send us your Spirit.)

1. We pray for all Christians. Lord Jesus, help your people to be generous to the poor.

2. We pray for our parish. Lord Jesus, please help us to be kind to new families.

3. We pray for ourselves. Lord Jesus, please help us to be happy in following you.

Pentecost 3

READING: Clash with the leaders (*New World* Pp168–169) Acts 3: 1; 4: 4.

Peter and John were walking one day up to the Temple. It was three o'clock in the afternoon, and people were gathering there for prayer.

In those days, a cripple whom everybody knew used to sit at one of the Temple gates—the 'Beautiful Gate'. He had been a cripple all his life, and his family put him there to beg from people as they were going into the Temple. This afternoon he was being carried to his pitch just as Peter and John came along. He caught sight of them and asked for money. They stopped.

'Look at us,' said Peter, watching him closely. He stared back at them both; he thought he was going to get something. 'I've no money,' said Peter, 'but I'll give you what I have: In the name of Jesus of Nazareth, get up and walk.'

He got hold of the man's hand and pulled him up. The man's feet and ankles became strong at once. He jumped about, stood still and walked around. Then he went into the Temple with Peter and John, now walking, now jumping, and thanking God all the time.

The crowd saw him walking round and thanking God. One after another they realised who he was. He was the beggar at the Temple Gate! They were amazed at what had happened to him. He kept holding onto Peter and John, and the people came crowding round them. By now they had got as far as Solomon's Porch; and when Peter saw what a crowd there was, he stood and faced them.

'Fellow countrymen,' he said, 'why does this surprise you? Why do you stare at us? There's nothing special about *us*; we didn't make this man walk about like this. It was his trust in Jesus that has made a healthy man of this beggar you all know so well.

'I know you really didn't know what you were doing when you treated Jesus as you did. But he is God's servant, and God raised him to life for your good, to get you to change your ways.'

At this moment the chief of police and some priests pushed their way in. They didn't want the friends of Jesus to talk to the people like this and tell them that Jesus was alive. They arrested Peter and John and took them off to prison for the night, for it was now getting dark.

The fact was that many of the people had taken Peter at his word—the number was reckoned at five thousand.

POINTS FOR CATECHIST

Read Barclay: Acts 3: 1; 4: 4.

This story shows the power of the Spirit at work in Peter. His faith and courage are in striking contrast with his weakness and cowardice only seven weeks previously. Peter no longer trusts in himself; he trusts in Jesus and gives him the glory. The anger of the police is understandable. Peter is preaching the power and the resurrection of Jesus, the man whom they were responsible for putting to death.

'It was his trust in Jesus'—other translations speak of faith in Jesus but do not specify whose faith.

PRESENTATION

1. Reading.

2. Help the children to enter into the feelings of the beggar. How would they feel if they (a) had been crippled all their lives;

(b) were totally dependent on others;

(c) had no hope of being cured;

(d) had to beg for a living?

Refer to places in the world today where the sick and cripples have no hope of being cured and have to beg for a living because of the scarcity of medical services and lack of any sick benefit.

3. How did the cripple react to his cure? Do we remember to thank God for his gifts, or do we take them for granted?

Which would you rather have, your health—or lots of money?

4. Has Peter changed since the night when he denied knowing Jesus? What has brought about this change? How did Peter feel when he cured the cripple?

5. Why were the leaders so upset and angry? How would you have felt in their situation? How do you think the crowds reacted?

ACT OF FAITH

Either sing:

He is Lord, He is Lord,
He is risen from the dead and He is Lord.

Every knee shall bow, every tongue confess
That Jesus Christ is Lord.

CCH 493.

Or

We believe in God the Father Almighty. We believe.

We believe in Jesus Christ, his only Son, our Lord. We believe.

We believe in the Holy Spirit, the Lord and Giver of Life. We believe.

BIDDING PRAYERS (Lord in your mercy, hear our prayer)

1. Lord Jesus, we pray for all disabled people, especially for any whom we know ... Please give them courage and trust in you.

2. Lord, Jesus, we pray for the sick and unemployed in our country. Please may they receive all the help they need.

3. Lord, Jesus, we pray for sick people in poor countries. May more hospitals be built and more doctors be trained, so that they may receive the care they need.

4. Lord, Jesus, we pray for those who have to beg for a living. Help them to keep their self respect, and make other people understanding and generous towards them.

Pentecost 4

READING: Prison Again (*New World*, Pp171–172). Acts 5: 12–42.

Peter and John and the other friends of Jesus went on telling the Good News. They met together in the Temple. Many people joined their company, and many sick people were cured.

The Jewish leaders were very angry about all this. So they arrested the friends of Jesus again and put them in the common prison. But they escaped during the night, and by dawn they were back in the Temple, telling the Good News again to the people there.

While this was happening, the High Priest and the Jewish leaders called the Council together, and sent for the prisoners. The police officers went to the prison, but the prisoners were no longer there. They went back without them. 'We found the prison safely locked all right,' they reported. 'The warders were on

guard at the doors. When we unlocked the doors, we found nobody inside.'

When the Chief Constable and the members of the Council heard this report, they had no idea what to do or what would happen next. Then someone came in with a report. 'The prisoners are back in the Temple, talking to the crowds,' he said.

The Chief Constable himself went to the Temple with police officers and brought them back to the court. They were very careful not to use any violence; they were afraid the crowd might start stoning them. The friends of Jesus faced the judges, and it was the High Priest who spoke.

'We gave you strict orders to stop talking about Jesus,' he said. 'Now everybody in the city is talking about him, and you're trying to make it look as if we were the people who killed him.'

'It's God's orders we must obey,' said Peter,

'not yours. The story we are telling is the plain truth. We are only talking about what we've seen for ourselves. God's power in us is proof of it too, the power he gives to all those who obey him.'

These words made them very angry and they wanted to pass the death sentence. But one of the members of the Council stood up—Gamaliel, a lawyer who was deeply respected by the people of the city. He ordered the prisoners out of the courtroom for a few minutes. 'My fellow-countrymen,' he said, 'be careful what you are about to do with these men. The point is this: keep your hands off these men and leave them alone. If this affair is just another popular uprising, it will come to nothing. If God is at the back of it, you can't stop these men—you'll be fighting against God himself.'

The Council agreed with him. They fetched the friends of Jesus back into court and had them flogged. They ordered them to stop talking about Jesus, and then set them free.

The friends of Jesus left the court happy men; happy because it was for telling the story of Jesus that they had been treated so shamefully. But they did not stop telling the people about him, either in the Temple or at home.

POINTS FOR CATECHIST:

Barclay: Acts 5: 12–42.

The transforming power of the Holy Spirit is evident; the Friends of Jesus are changed men. They are now so eager to spread the message that Jesus is alive that nothing can deter them. Their own safety is forgotten in their desire to do what God wants.

The anger of the leaders is understandable. They realised that the message preached by Peter and the disciples would undermine their own teaching and position of authority.

PRESENTATION:

1. Reading.

2. 'The leaders were very angry about all *this*'.—Discuss . . .

> the preaching about Jesus;
> curing the sick in Jesus' name;
> so many people joining the friends of Jesus;

the friends of Jesus meeting in the Temple.

The leaders were afraid of losing their power and authority. How do we feel when we are shown to be in the wrong? Do we feel jealous if others are chosen instead of us? How do we react?

3. They were put in the common prison. Ask the children if they know anything about prisons in those days. The common prison was normally one room with a stone floor, no furniture, no sanitation, and little or no air. Prisoners had no privacy, no exercise and very poor food.

4. The friends of Jesus left the court happy men. Why? Help the children reflect on their experience of the happiness which can come simply from knowing that we are doing right. Do they notice a change in these men since the coming of the Spirit at Pentecost?

5. *9–10 years*: 'If God is at the back of it you can't stop these men.' Show how Gamaliel's prophecy has proved to be true throughout the ages. The Church grows when there is persecution.

ACT OF FAITH

SOS 98 'How great is our God'; *or CCH* 444 'Do not be afraid.'

Lord Jesus Christ help us

> to know you more clearly
> to love you more dearly
> and to follow you more nearly, day by day.

BIDDING PRAYERS (Lord, send them your Spirit.)

1. Lord Jesus, we pray for people who are in prison because they love you. Please comfort them with your Spirit.

2. Lord Jesus, we pray for bishops and priests in countries which are against Christians. Please give them wisdom and courage.

3. Lord Jesus, we pray for leaders who are against your Church. Please open their hearts to your Spirit of truth.

Pentecost 5

READING: Trouble Again (*New World*, Pp188–189). Acts 12: 1–19.

Herod again arrested some of the friends of Jesus. He had James, the brother of John, beheaded. This made him popular. So he looked around for others, and, during the Great Feast, arrested Peter as well.

After his arrest, he put him in prison with sixteen soldiers on guard. He planned to parade him before the people when the feast was over. All the friends of Jesus could do was pray for him, and this they did day and night. The feast was over and the very next day Herod had planned to bring Peter out and show him to the crowds. It was late at night. Peter was asleep. Two soldiers lay on either side of him and he was handcuffed to them. Outside the prison door, sentries stood on guard.

A light shone in the cell and a messenger from God stood there. He tapped Peter on his side and woke him up. 'Get up quickly,' he said. The handcuffs fell from his wrists. 'Fasten your belt,' he said, 'and put your sandals on.' Peter did what he was told. 'Put your cloak on and follow me.' Peter followed him out.

It was like a dream; it didn't seem real. They passed the first sentry, then the second sentry, and came to the great iron gate. Beyond the gate lay the city. Nobody was there, but the gate swung open. They went through, and along the narrow street. The messenger vanished.

By this time Peter was wide awake. 'Now I know God has rescued me,' he said to himself; 'rescued me from Herod and the show the crowds were looking forward to.'

He realised what had happened, and went off to the house of Mary, John Mark's mother, where many friends of Jesus were meeting to pray for him. He knocked on the door of the outer gate, and Rhoda, a maid, came to see who it was. She knew at once it was Peter's voice. Back she ran to tell everybody—she didn't stop to open the door, she was so happy.

'Peter's outside the door,' she burst out. 'You're mad,' they told her. 'It *is* Peter,' said Rhoda, 'It's his ghost,' they said. Peter went on knocking.

At last they went and opened the door—and to their amazement, there was Peter himself. With a wave of his hand, he got them to be quiet, and told them how God had rescued him from prison. 'Tell James and the other friends of Jesus,' he said. Then he left them and went away.

There was great alarm among the soldiers when daylight came. They hadn't any idea what had become of Peter. Herod ordered a search for him, but he was nowhere to be found. He had the guards examined and ordered them to be executed.

Then he went down from Jerusalem to his palace at Caesarea.

POINTS FOR CATECHIST

Barclay: Acts 12: 1–19.

Herod killed James and arrested Peter, not for reasons of justice or for a religious principle, but simply to curry favour with the leaders of the people. Peter, in his position as leader, was a great prize. This Herod was grandson of Herod the Great.

In this passage, the 'Angel of the Lord' is translated 'a messenger of God'. Angels always symbolise the presence of God, and this escape is clearly the work of God—in answer to the prayer of the community.

The James mentioned at the end of the passage was leader or bishop of the Christian community in Jerusalem. Matthew's Gospel refers to him as a 'brother of the Lord', ie, a cousin or relative of Jesus. He is the author of St James' Epistle and was martyred around AD 62.

PRESENTATION:

1. Reading.

2. Let the children comment on Herod's actions at (a) the beginning and (b) the end of the story.

   Why did he choose to parade Peter before the people?

   Why did he order such strict security?

3. Why were the friends of Jesus shattered by Peter's arrest? How did they try to help him? Might some people have laughed and said: 'What's the good of praying, why don't you *do* something?' Were they right to believe in the power of prayer? When things go wrong for us, do we turn to God in prayer?

4. Try to imagine how Peter felt:

(a) so securely guarded;
(b) when God's messenger came to him.

He didn't understand what was happening, but he trusted in God and obeyed his directions.

Supposing he had questioned the directions. What would have happened then?

God can do great things for us if we trust and obey him. We can't always see the reasons for what God wants, until much later.

5. Imagine (a) the joy of Rhoda and the Friends of Jesus; and (b) Peter's feelings—freed by God and now left on the doorstep to be captured again!

ACT OF FAITH:

CCH 457 chorus, 'Fear not, rejoice and be glad'; *or* 'Our Father, who art in heaven, hallowed be Thy name, Thy Kingdom come, Thy will be done'.

BIDDING PRAYERS (Lord in your mercy, hear our prayer.)

1. Lord Jesus, we pray for the Pope, and for the leaders of all Christian churches. May your Holy Spirit of Wisdom guide them.

2. Lord Jesus, we pray for ourselves and our families. Please give us a spirit of prayer.

3. Lord Jesus, we pray for the leaders of our country. Please open their hearts to your Spirit of Wisdom.

Pentecost 6

READING: Stephen's arrest (*New World*, Pp177–180, adapted.) Acts 6 and 7.

There were many Jewish people in Jerusalem City who had not been born in Palestine. They had come from their homes in such faraway places as North Africa and Asia. They spoke Greek and read the Bible in Greek. Many were freed slaves or the sons of freed slaves. They had their own meeting house in the city where they met together to worship God—the Freedman's Meeting House. Most of them had come on pilgrimage.

Some of these Jewish people had joined the company of the friends of Jesus; and their leader was Stephen, a man who spoke, as Jesus had spoken, with such charm and power that people felt they had to listen. Stephen told the Good News to these Jewish people from overseas in their meeting house. Many of them got up and argued with him, but they could not answer *his* arguments. He spoke sensibly and with God's *power*.

So they made secret plans. They spread rumours about him. Finally they arrested him and took him to court. Stephen then spoke to the Council, and he had a lot to say.

'Only the world is big enough for God, and we must live in his *way*. But you Jewish people are always the same, as the Bible makes clear—you will never listen to God. You are just the same as your ancestors. Is there any man of God your ancestors did not treat badly? They even killed the Men of God, although they were explaining God's Way and telling them how one day he would send his chosen leader.

In our own day God has sent his chosen leader, and all you could do was to hand him over to the Romans and have him killed—you whom God himself has taught but who never did what he told you.'

They had listened quietly to him so far, but these last words made them wild with anger and they hissed at him. Stephen himself was filled with God's power and gazed over their heads. All he was thinking about and all he could see was Jesus, full of God's glory and full of God's power.

'I see God's throne in heaven,' he said, 'and Jesus at God's right hand.' The whole crowd broke into a great uproar. They pressed their hands to their ears to shut out the sound of his voice; and in one great rush they tumbled over one another to get at him.

They dragged him outside the city to stone him to death. The men whose duty it was to see that he was really dead brought their clothes and put them down before a young officer of the court called Saul.

'Lord Jesus, receive me,' Stephen kept praying, even while they were throwing the stones at him. He knelt down on the ground. 'O God,' he called out, 'forgive them this great wrong they are doing.'

It was all over. Saul was quite sure the right thing had been done.

That wasn't all that happened on that day, either. The crowds went off to get hold of other friends of Jesus like Stephen, but they escaped into the country districts of Judea and Samaria.

The close friends of Jesus like Peter and John were left alone. But Saul wanted more than the death of one man; he wanted to get rid of all the friends of Jesus. He went from house to house, and dragged men and women off to prison.

POINTS FOR CATECHIST

Barclay: Acts 6 and 7.

The word martyr means witness. Martyrs witness, by their death, to the faith they believe in. Stephen is the first Christian martyr. He mirrors Jesus both in his preaching and in his death.

PRESENTATION

1. Reading.

2. Stephen wanted to share his Good News with outsiders, newcomers to Jerusalem. What is your attitude to new children, or to those outside your own group of friends?

3. Why were the people angered by Stephen's preaching? How would you have felt if you had been listening to him? Do you get angry and take it out on others when you are told off about your behaviour or your work?

'We must live in his Way.' Do you ever feel obstinate when you are told to change your ways?

4. Do you know (a) what a martyr is; (b) the name of the first Christian martyr; (c) the names of any other martyrs and how they died; (d) whether there are martyrs in the world today?

Could Stephen and these other martyrs have saved themselves? Where did their courage come from?

Do we find it easy to stand up for what is right? Do we ask the Holy Spirit to help us?

5. Which words of Stephen remind us of Jesus? Do you find it difficult to forgive others when they treat you badly? Does it take courage to forgive?

6. *7–8 years*: What do you like most about this story? A discussion on this could take up the whole session

ACT OF FAITH

We believe that God is the Father of everyone. We believe.

We believe that Jesus came to save everyone. We believe.

We believe that Jesus gives his Spirit to all who ask for his help. We believe.

BIDDING PRAYERS (Lord Jesus, give us your Spirit.)

1. Dear Jesus, please help us to be like you in forgiving those who hurt us.

2. Dear Jesus, please help us to be brave in standing up for what is right.

3. Dear Jesus, please help us to listen to you.

Pentecost 7

READING: Saul on the Road (*New World*, Pp190–192). Acts 9: 1–18.

Saul was hot on the trail of the friends of Jesus, thirsting for their blood. He went to the High Priest and asked him for warrants to search the Meeting Houses in Damascus, to arrest all 'the people of God's Way'—as the friends of Jesus called themselves, and to bring them, men and women alike, as prisoners to Jerusalem City. He set off along the Damascus Road. He had almost reached his journey's end when, suddenly, a light from the sky burst on him and he fell down on the road. He heard a voice.

'Saul, Saul,' the voice called. 'Why do you treat me like an enemy?' 'Who are you?' asked Saul. 'I am Jesus—and you are treating me like an enemy. But get up and go on into Damascus City. You'll get your orders there.'

His fellow-travellers stood speechless with fright. They heard the voice, but they saw nobody. Saul got up. When he tried to see where he was, he found he was blind; they had to lead him by the hand into the city. For three days he was blind and had nothing to eat or drink.

A friend of Jesus, Ananias, was living in Damascus City. He had a dream, and in the dream he saw Jesus. 'Ananias,' said Jesus. 'I'm here, Lord,' he answered. 'Get up,' said Jesus, 'and go to Straight Street. Find the house where Judas lives, and ask for Saul, a citizen of Tarsus City. You'll find him praying. He's had a dream, and in his dream he has seen a man called Ananias enter the house and put his hands on his eyes and give him his sight back again.'

'Lord,' said Ananias, 'I've heard all sorts of stories about this man; he's here with a warrant to arrest all your friends in the city.'

'Off you go,' said Jesus. 'I've marked him out as my messenger. His orders are to tell the whole world the Good News—foreigners and their governments as well as Jewish people. And I'll not hide from him the dangers he'll have to face as a friend of mine.'

Ananias went off and found the house and put his hands on Saul. 'Brother Saul,' he said, 'It was the Lord Jesus you saw on the road outside the city. He has sent me to you. May you have your sight back again, and may you be filled with God's power.'

His sight came back—as suddenly as he had lost it—and he could see quite clearly. He got up, and Ananias baptised him and received him into the company of the friends of Jesus. He had a good meal and felt quite well again.

POINTS FOR CATECHIST

Barclay: Acts 9: 1–18.

Jesus chooses the most unexpected people for his work. Perhaps he saw how he could use Saul's single-mindedness. Jesus' words to Saul reflect the teaching of his ministry: 'Whatever you do to the most unimportant person, you do to me.'

We don't know exactly what Saul experienced. Others heard sounds but saw nothing. Although his conversion appears sudden, he may have been reflecting on Stephen's sermon, on his courage and on his forgiveness of his enemies.

PRESENTATION

1. Refer briefly to last week's story and Saul's place in it.

   Reading.

2. Discuss:
   (a) Why was Saul going to Damascus? What kind of a person was he? Why do you think Jesus chose him?
   (b) What did Jesus mean when he said: 'Why do you treat me like an enemy?' (This is a difficult concept for children.)
   (c) Why do you think Saul was blinded? Was it to show him he was blind to God's truth? We say: 'Oh, I see!' when something is explained clearly to us. Perhaps Saul suddenly realised how blind he'd been.

3. What do you learn about Ananias from (a) the way he reacted to the call of Jesus; and (b) the way he called Saul his brother?

How would you have felt towards Ananias if you were Saul?

How would you have felt towards Saul if you were Ananias?

How can Saul and Ananias help us in our following of Jesus? What can we learn from them?

4. Are we sometimes like Ananias, sometimes like Saul, when God asks things of us?

ACT OF FAITH

Lord, we believe in you. Increase our faith.
Lord, we trust in you. Increase our hope.
Lord, we love you. Help us to love you, more and more.
CCH 477, chorus: 'Freely, freely ...'; *or AK* 82 'Sing alleluia'.

BIDDING PRAYERS (Lord Jesus, give them your Spirit.)

1. Lord Jesus, we pray for those who are blind to the truth. Please help them to believe in you.

2. Lord Jesus, we pray for those who treat your friends badly. Please change their hearts.

3. Lord Jesus, we pray for those who are afraid to answer your call. Please give them courage and strength.

Pentecost 8

READING: Saul meets the Friends of Jesus. (*New World*, Pp192–194.) Acts 9: 19–30.

Saul stayed with the friends of Jesus for a few days. The first thing he did was to go along to the meeting house and tell them the story of Jesus.

'He *is* God's Son,' he said.

Everybody listening to him talk was amazed. 'Isn't this the man who tried to wipe out the friends of Jesus in Jerusalem City?' they asked. 'Why, he came here with a warrant for the arrest of those who live here, to take them back as prisoners to our leaders.'

This didn't stop Saul. He spoke all the more powerfully in the meeting houses. He shocked the Jewish people in the city. They didn't know how to answer his arguments. He had only one thing to say: Jesus is God's chosen leader.

This went on for quite a time. At last the Jewish people plotted to murder him, and they picketed the city gates the whole twenty-four hours of the day. Somebody told Saul about the plot; and one night his friends took him to the city wall and lowered him over the wall in a basket.

Saul went back to Jerusalem. He tried to get in touch with the friends of Jesus there; but they were afraid of him. They thought he was just pretending to be a friend of Jesus.

But Barnabas introduced him to the Christian leaders. He told them how Saul had seen Jesus on the Damascus Road and been given his orders, and how he had told the Good News boldly in the meeting houses of Damascus City.

That settled it, and he was welcomed into all their homes.

He showed the same boldness in talking about Jesus in Jerusalem City as he had in Damascus City. His chief aim was to meet the Jews from overseas and argue with them, but like the Damascus Jews, they made up their minds to murder him.

Somebody told the friends of Jesus about the plot, and they took him down to the port of Caesarea and sent him off home to Tarsus City.

POINTS FOR CATECHIST

Barclay: Acts 9: 19–30.

This session must be closely linked with Saul's conversion. Within a few days of receiving back his sight, Saul is preaching about Jesus in the Damascus synagogue. No wonder the people were amazed.

'This went on for quite a time.' Saul spent about three years in the city. We see the power of the Holy Spirit at work, teaching him what to say and giving him both eloquence and courage.

We owe a debt of gratitude to Barnabas, who befriended Saul, trusting him when other Christians were afraid to accept him into their company. Paul's letter, No 5, shows what happened to him subsequently.

PRESENTATION

1. Refer to last week's reading. Read the passage.

2. Why were the people in the meeting house amazed to hear Saul preaching about

Jesus? If you had been there, would you have felt suspicious and wondered if it were a trap?

3. Would it have been easy for Saul to change his way of life? How do we know that many of his friends turned against him? Do you feel lonely and miserable if a friend turns against you?

   How did Saul know what to preach about Jesus? Did he need courage?

   Who gave him the help he needed?

   Do you ever ask the Holy Spirit to help you when you are upset or in difficulty?

4. Did the friends of Jesus in Jerusalem trust Saul? How would you feel if someone who had been horrid to you, suddenly wanted to be your friend? What would you *do*?

   Who befriended Saul and brought him into the group? How would Saul feel towards Barnabas? From now on Saul used his Roman name—Paul—to show that he was a different kind of person.

5. If time, *Listen!* P159, No 79B, extract from a Letter of St Paul:

   Dear Friends,
   These are some of the things that have happened to me while I have been telling people about Jesus. I have had to work very hard. I've been sent to prison, I've been beaten up (in fact I was nearly killed once). I've been shipwrecked (and once I was lost at sea all night).

   I've always been on the move and I've often been afraid that I was going to be attacked by bandits. I've had to get across rivers when there's been no bridge to walk over. I've often had to go on working without going to bed all night. Sometimes I've been so hungry and thirsty that I've nearly died.

   Once I even had some soldiers chasing me and I had to get away by hiding in a basket and my friends lowered me out of their window over the city walls so that I could escape and go free.

   Nevertheless I can put up with all this, because I am doing it all for the sake of Jesus.

ACT OF FAITH

Lord Jesus Christ,
Help us to know you more clearly
Love you more dearly
and follow you more nearly, day by day.

CCH 477, Chorus, 'Freely, freely . . .'

BIDDING PRAYERS (Lord Jesus, give them your spirit.)

1. Lord Jesus, we pray for people who have just become Christians. Please fill them with your love.

2. Lord Jesus, we pray for people who have been in prison and are starting a new life. Please give them courage and strength.

3. Lord Jesus, we pray for people who are lonely and without friends. Please bless and comfort them.

CHRISTMAS TIME IS COMING

From: Lord, Hear Us by Sr Mary Oswin
Published by Geoffrey Chapman
Reprinted with permission

ADVENT SONG

From: Let God's Children Sing by Sr Mary Oswin
Published by Geoffrey Chapman
Reprinted with permission

QUESTION AND ANSWER CAROL

From: Let God's Children Sing by Sr Mary Oswin
Published by Geoffrey Chapman
Reprinted with permission